benny blanco

with
jess damuck

photographs by
johnny miller

DEYST.

An Imprint of WILLIAM MORROW

open wide

a cookbook for friends

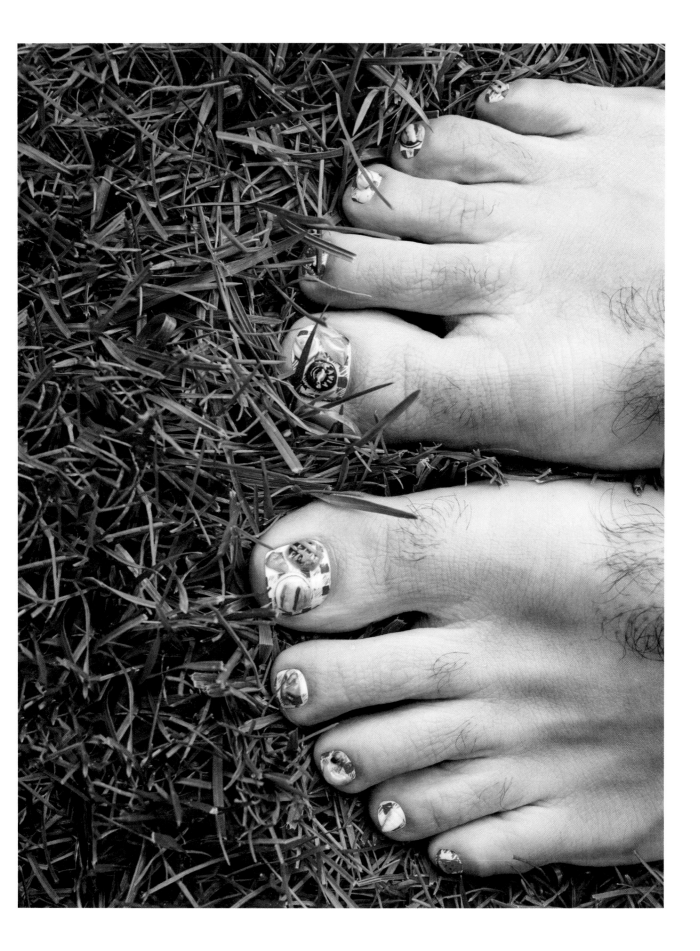

hi, i'm benny blanco

I'm five foot five on a good day. I love eating, sex, music, and taking the perfect shit. At any given moment they are all fighting for the number one spot. I'm in a television show with my best friend, Dave, I own a record label and am a recording artist, and I probably produced most of the songs you have heard on the radio from 2008 until now (which is ironic because I didn't even grow up listening to pop music).

I grew up in Virginia with my mom, who mostly ate almonds and scrambled eggs. I didn't even try sushi until I was eighteen, and going out to eat was so rare I'm not even sure if it ever happened (but if it did it probably involved a Bloomin' Onion). My mom worked in another state and was constantly juggling a slew of men she had just met on JDate, so most nights for dinner I'd get creative on my own.

When I was thirteen, my friend got a George Foreman Grill and it changed my life forever. We would invite friends over, get stoned, and make the most elaborate sandwiches our prepubescent minds could fathom.

I became obsessed with food and cooking for friends. I would befriend every chef I met, buy every dumb kitchen gadget I could find on Amazon, and travel hours for food. If every meal didn't end with some version of "This is the best meal I've ever had in my entire life!" I was depressed.

Not that much has changed since my George Foreman climax except a few hit singles, my testicles dropping, and an insane ten-foot-wide pizza oven in my backyard decorated with mosaic tiles that spell BLANCO.

I still get the same feeling when I walk out of my kitchen and see my friends awaiting my creations, but now instead of bad sandwiches I bring out a freezing cold dish filled with toro and uni topped with generous spoonfuls of caviar.

For a second let's pretend it's *you* who just cocked your head back. The moment the toro hits your tongue it starts to melt away like butter. Its richness lasts only a second before a briny wave of creamy decadence pulls you into an invigorating breath of the sea. The pop of caviar bursts intense bits of salty water in your mouth, and, with your eyes closed, you swear you can actually hear the ocean.

As you begin to get your bearings, you look around and you're surrounded

by people. Some faces are familiar, but most you don't recognize. You turn to your right and see a woman in her late sixties wearing a bedazzled bikini that says I LOVE NY, who is carrying a kugel in a casserole dish (that's Sandy, my mom). The smells are intoxicating. You wonder how many days I've been smoking the wagyu tenderloins that are about to come off the grill. You spark up a conversation with a man who smoked resin scraped off the back of a toad last week and keeps asking you, "What does it all mean?" A magical woman walks by and you get a strong whiff of vanilla and spices. She's speaking French to the beautiful baby she's holding in one arm, while she pours an orange wine from Mexico with the other hand. The baby eats a small sliver of hay-wrapped pecorino someone just brought home from a vacation in Siena and giggles. You're starting to get full but I convince you to eat your last bite of truffle smashed potatoes in my jacuzzi. I then spin you into the sauna and you emerge right before you actually start to melt, but then you are passed a joint the size of a baseball bat and a plate of banana pudding. It's almost all too much. You see the softest velvet couch ever and sink into the corner, which is covered with stuffed animals. Someone tosses one aside and lets you know they are actually pieces of art. The music begins to shift and it sounds like it is coming from the other room. Home seems too far away. Should you just have one more scoop of banana pudding and sneak into a guest bedroom?

No one will notice if you're gone for a few hours. You'll tell all your friends about the party in the morning but they won't believe you until you bring them to one to see for themselves. And, *bammmmmmmm!* We're now back to reality and you're just sitting on your couch reading the introduction to my book.

I KNOW WHAT YOU ARE GOING TO SAY, and I get it. Cooking is scary. You don't know where to begin. It can be overwhelming. And cooking for a group of people, forget about it. But I promise you, once you get into it, it will be your new addiction. I work like twenty hours a day but somehow manage to cook two or three meals—it's not a chore, it's something I look forward to. Whether I'm cooking for fifteen people or just for myself, there is something meditative about it. Slicing an onion is like taking a Xanax to me.

A lot of cookbooks call for insane ingredients, prep times, and experience. This is more of a plug and play type of book. Yes, there are a few things you may have to look up, but I tried to make this easy because I like easy. Scratch that. I like it to look like it was hard but be easy to execute.

We put so much importance on our own success, using it to try to justify whether we are happy or not, when all we really need is a little warm focaccia right out of the oven and a good conversation. I encourage you to slow down, have a dinner party, invite your friends, and tell them to

invite their friends. You'll be amazed that pretty much any combination of people you put together (most likely) works out. Unless your friend is an asshole (then you don't have to invite them again). It's not about spending a ton of money on lavish ingredients. Sometimes we just eat Domino's and lava cakes until we puke. Try cooking something from scratch though. And if you can't cook (you'll be able to after this book), ask your friends to bring something or make something simple. It's about bringing people you love together.

Whenever I'm throwing a dinner party, I get this strange feeling in my belly the whole time (but it's a good kind of strange, like the butterflies just before you lean in for a first kiss, or when you look the wrong way before you cross the street and almost get hit by a car). My life is so fast-paced and every day I experience things that sound like stories the pathological liar kid in your third-grade class made up. But that's not what life's about to me. I crave the teeny memories that happen in between the big stuff. Like watching kids run out of my kitchen with candy stuffed in their pockets while saying their first curse words. Or two people falling in love while my dog Larry licks their legs until there is no

cocoa butter lotion left on their bodies. Or watching a seventy-six-year-old man lose himself and find himself all over again in the course of a single night.

I wrote this book to teach you everything I know about food, cooking, and throwing the greatest dinner party of all time. I'll show you how to create the vibe, prep a perfect dinner, execute it, and leave everyone wondering when they'll be invited back for the next one. Use this book as your handbook and you're going to slam dunk with your tongue out like MJ and leave your nuts in the competition's mouth. Hopefully just figuratively, unless it's some kind of sex party, in which case I'd like an invitation.

I've been told some of the finest stories over meals. I've laughed so hard I thought I was going to actually die. I've fallen in love—sometimes with the food, sometimes with the person across the table. I've cried in good ways, and I've cried in bad ways. I hope you've been lucky enough to have all these same memories and then some. But if you haven't, I can make you a promise. If you follow these three simple steps, it will all become a reality: Open this book. Open your heart. And open wide, baby.

i guess you're wondering what this book's about

This book is broken down into a few sections. There are all the basics to get your kitchen ready, a little set-up advice from my "expert" friends, and then all of the dinner party menus I love to make.

I'm so relieved to finally have this book for my friends to buy instead of having to text them recipes all the time. You don't have to make every single item to have a great party, but my menus will take the guessing out of what goes together. If it seems like too much work, buy your friend the book so they can bring a dish and make it a potluck. Some of the dishes take a few minutes, others take a few days. Be sure to read through the recipes first and get all the groceries you need. I promise everyone's going to be so happy.

I've also written a list of my top places to eat in New York and Los Angeles with some actual recipes from my favorite spots, including a secret recipe from Carbone.

Then there are a bunch of random recipes that didn't fit into the menus but are way too good not to be in here, like the cake from my BTS music video and a Rolex from Ed Sheeran that I deep-fried. I don't know why they let me make a cookbook.

After the party, I'll show you how to make cleanup a more enjoyable experience as well as how to kick out your friends (or people you barely know) without making them mad.

Grab a napkin, roll up your sleeves, and let's fuck.

benny's little cooking tips

1. **HAVE FUN.** We are making food, not performing open heart surgery. Play some music. Smoke a joint. Relax. Take your time.

2. **DON'T BE ANXIOUS.** You don't have to check the fish every two seconds. It's going to cook. Don't let the anxiety get in the food because you can taste it, and it doesn't taste good.

3. **IT'S THE THOUGHT THAT COUNTS.** You are making a meal for someone. So even if it tastes bad it doesn't matter because you took your time and tried your best.

4. **DON'T LET A RECIPE OVERWHELM YOU.** It doesn't have to be exact. I'm not expecting you to be Gordon Ramsay on your first try. If you feel like putting something in or taking it out, do it, but if it sucks don't blame me. LOL. But seriously, just be you, get creative.

5. **DON'T MAKE COOKING A CHORE.** Take your time. Cooking is one of the few moments I can slow down and just focus on what I'm doing, like thinly slicing vegetables, picking herbs for a garnish, or making sure I added the right amount of turmeric. It's like meditating when you do it the right way.

6. **SEASON YOUR FUCKING FOOD.** My mom always gets mad because I put so much salt on everything. She doesn't realize that when she's at a restaurant, the reason it tastes good is because they're so heavy handed.

my kitchen

I find it interesting when I'm at a friend's place and they have nothing to cook with. My friend Dave, aka Lil' Dicky, has the exact kitchen an eight-year-old would have if you gave him $1,000 and said, "Time to stock the kitchen." It has your basic pots and pans, but it's mostly pasta, rice, and cereal. Some of my friends don't even have a knife to cut a lemon. There are so many pantry staples that are shortcuts to things tasting amazing and tools that can level-up your cooking tenfold. Use this section as a kitchen guide, but by no means a bible. You have to find the things that work for you and the spices that tickle your fancy. Hopefully this is only the beginning of your culinary journey.

PRODUCE

Buy your vegetables at the farmers market. If you can't get to the market, make sure any produce that has a skin, like a berry or a tomato, is organic. Check out CSAs in your area and other delivery options like Misfits Market. If you really want fresh produce, you should do what I do and grow it yourself; but I'm warning you, what started out as some herbs on a windowsill has turned into me utilizing every square inch of my property to create my own little farm. It's always been my dream to live on a ranch with fourteen dogs, livestock, and wildflowers that make me want to skip around and sing "Oh, oh it's magic, you know." Me and my garden fairy Scott started growing so many vegetables that

I couldn't eat them all. Now we provide food for areas without access to fresh foods around LA. For scale, we're producing about one hundred pounds of vegetables a week. So suck on my green thumb, baby.

HOT SAUCE

I love hot sauce. Sometimes I use so much hot sauce that you can't even see the food underneath and my lips start to chafe. These are the hot sauces I have at all times. I use different sauces for different dishes.

Calabrian chile spread/paste: This amazing fiery paste is made from blended Calabrian chiles, garlic, and olive oil. You can even find it at Trader Joe's now.

Cholula Green Pepper sauce: Love this on anything Mexican or Tex-Mex, not too spicy.

Crystal: Vinegar-based hot sauce I use for my soul food cooking.

Frank's RedHot: The *classic*. Can't live without it. You'll literally use an entire bottle in my Microwave Buffalo Chicken Nachos on page 263.

Jah Mama: Liquid gold. My friend Jah makes this amazing pepper sauce that you'll want to drink by the bottle, but don't do it because it's fucking hot.

Sriracha: Garlicky, savory, spicy perfection.

Tabasco: Another vinegar-based hot sauce, perfect for adding to sauces and marinades or just adding a dash of heat.

Valentina: A must-have for tacos.

Yamajirushi Yuzu-it: A Japanese yuzu-flavored sauce that is perfect for an everyday hot sauce.

Yuzu koshu: More of a paste than a sauce. This is a citrusy, spicy, salty, completely insane one you'll want to swim in, but don't do it because that would be painful. Use sparingly.

Zab's: I love Zab's. It's made from datil peppers and contributes the perfect amount of heat.

SPICES

These are my favorite spices. You can cut corners in some areas of your kitchen to save money, but investing in high-quality spices changed my life because now everything is, without fail, blow-your-mind insanely flavorful every single time I cook. When I started buying spices at SOS Chefs in New York, it was like I was tasting things for the first time. Also, no one tells you this, but spices go bad after like a year. Some of these are fancy and you'll only use them once a year but a lot of them you'll use every day. Other great online spice retailers are Burlap & Barrel, Diaspora, and I always like to see what Noma Projects is making.

The Basics

Black peppercorn: Always buy whole peppercorns and invest in a good grinder or mortar and pestle. Sometimes I keep some already ground in a little bowl, but when you grind it fresh it has so much amazing flavor. It's insane how much pepper can enhance a dish.

Chef Paul Prudhomme's Poultry Magic: One of my friend Pop's favorite seasoning blends.

Chili flakes: A quality chili flake adds heat to sauces and stews and is the perfect finish on a slice of pizza. Once you have your basic chili flakes, you can branch out with something like smoky Urfa chili or a more mild silk chili.

Cinnamon Toast Crunch Cinnadust: Vanilla, graham-crackery, cinnamon-sugary flavor blast to sprinkle on everything. You need this for French Toast on page 185.

Coriander (ground): Coriander is the seed of the cilantro plant and has a similar flavor but is less intense. It is the base of so many different cuisines from Tex-Mex to Middle Eastern. It has a great citrusy flavor and is usually paired with cumin, so get both.

Cumin (ground): Cumin's warm and bitter flavor is an important ingredient in so many cuisines. Toasting it in the pan a little mellows out the intensity.

Lawry's Seasoned Salt: Lawry's is a blend of a bunch of different spices like paprika, garlic, onion, and celery. It will flavor-blast anything you put it in.

Old Bay Seasoning: If you're cooking seafood, you need Old Bay on hand. Period.

Onion powder and garlic powder: These are chilled-out versions of the real thing, with no chopping required. Great for seasoning in dry rubs or stirring into sauces and marinades.

Oregano: This is one of those herbs that tastes better dried. No pizza sauce is complete without it.

Paprika: Smoked, sweet, or hot. Paprika is the perfect way to add a little something to the base of any dish. I like to have all three on hand for different dishes. It's a great way to add some color, too.

All the salts: I use Diamond Crystal Kosher Salt for almost everything in this book because it's the perfect size for seasoning. A good flaky salt like Maldon is essential too, for when you want to finish a steak or something with that perfect little crunch.

Sesame seeds: I buy these already toasted from the Japanese supermarket and sprinkle them on everything.

Taco seasoning: I probably eat a thousand tacos a year. This indispensable spice blend has chili powder, cumin, coriander, and more. I like mine spicy.

Tony Chachere's Famous Creole Cuisine No Salt Seasoning Blend: My friend Pop uses this seasoning in his fried chicken and collard greens for an extra boost of flavor.

Turmeric: It's peppery, kind of gingery, and so bright yellow it will stain everything you own. I love it in curries and dressings.

Get a Little Fancy

Once you start moving beyond the basics you can really start to have fun with new

flavors. These aren't absolutely necessary, but they are nice to have on hand.

Cardamom: I like to buy the whole pods and use them to flavor the Indian-inspired cooking I do. Cardamom is a hard flavor to describe. It's sweet and a little bit like licorice. You crush the pods and just use the little seeds inside.

Fennel (seed): Grind up these little licorice-y seeds and use them in rubs and marinades.

Garam masala: A delicious Indian spice blend with cumin, coriander, cardamom, cinnamon, mace, and peppercorns ready for curries and more.

Kashmiri chili powder: This is a mild North Indian chili.

Nigella seeds: These are like super-powered onion sprinkles.

Nobu Dry Miso Seasoning: Adds amazing umami flavor to anything it's sprinkled on.

Pink peppercorns: Pink peppercorns are my favorite thing. You might not use them every day, but when you do they are magical, like tiny blasts of fruit, flowers, and spice.

Saffron: It's expensive but a little goes a long way. If you put too much in, it tastes like a mixture of toilet and bong water.

Sumac: A sour candy–level liquid-lemon tartness in powder form.

SOS Chefs Vadouvan Curry powder and Coconut Milk Powder: This super-special combination makes the most insane curry sauce ever.

Yuzu Shichimi: You'll find this in the Shrimp Katsu Sandwiches. I know this sounds like a lot of yuzu in my book but they all have a different place. And yuzu is amazing. Don't knock it till you try it.

Yuzu-flavored togarashi: I use this as an everyday spice. It requires a trip to a Japanese market, but it's so worth it. It's the best sprinkle of heat.

SAUCES

Sauces are drippy blankets of flavor that you tuck the dish into bed with before putting it in your mouth. Sometimes I dip. Sometimes I drown. I don't think I've ever met a sauce I didn't like, but here are a few of my favorites that you'll find in various recipes throughout the book.

Cocktail Sauce (page 49)

Tartar Sauce (page 53)

Zhoug (page 60)

White Sauce (page 62)

Marinara Sauce (page 68)

Chimichurri Sauce (page 120)

Queso (page 121)

Matty's Burger Sauce (page 241)

Quesadilla Sauce (page 261)

FATS

Fat is how you make your food taste good. It releases and concentrates flavors. I always hear this talk about what oils will kill you or not. I haven't done the research so you

might die eating some of these, but you'll have a pretty great meal as you take your final breaths.

Beef tallow: Rendered beef fat has a mild beefy flavor that I love. It also has a high smoke point, so it's perfect for frying. McDonald's used to fry their French fries in it, so you know it's an addictive taste.

Mayo: Duke's and Kewpie are my favorites. You can make your own mayonnaise with egg yolks and oil, but buying a good jar of it is way easier and honestly tastes better.

Olive oil: My favorite olive oils are extra virgin olive oils from Sicily. I love the oil from my friends Nino (Partanna) and Pia (Baroncini Imports). Look for olive oil from a single region, not blends with olives from all over the world. Extra virgin olive oil means it's the best quality,

so always go for that, even if it's more expensive.

Peanut oil: Another with a high smoke point for frying. Great for using as a neutral-flavored oil when cooking dishes that don't require a stronger-flavored fat like olive oil or tallow.

Unsalted butter: Always use unsalted butter for cooking so you can season it yourself. Sometimes I keep fancy salted butter around for bread, though.

MY FAVORITE THINGS

Things in Jars, Bottles, and Cans
Anchovies: I sneak these into my food wherever and whenever I can. Everyone always says they don't like anchovies but really everyone does. It's that extra salty savory punch in your mouth that

pastas and sauces need. For topping salads or making little toasts, I like to use boquerones, or white anchovies. They have a milder, sweeter flavor.

Bachan's Japanese Barbecue Sauce: I love this sticky tangy spicy sauce.

Biscoff spread: Literally cookies ground into a paste, need I say more?

Rooted Fare Crunchy Black Sesame Butter: I can't believe this is legal and heroine is illegal. They must be made of the same thing.

Chili crisp: You can make your own chili crisp, but you can buy it too. S&B's Crunchy Garlic and Fly by Jing are my favorites. Sometimes I use my fingers to eat it out of the jar, but don't touch your eyes or your peepee after . . . it's spicy.

Dr. Dane's Kitchen Authentic Vietnamese Lemongrass Chili Sauce and Dr. Dane's Kitchen Authentic Vietnamese Dipping Sauce: Keep these two sauces on hand for smothering on veggies and meats and dipping just about anything in.

Gochujang: Spicy-sticky-sweet-boi. Korean chili paste.

Miso: Miso *is* umami. I add the paste to soup, dressings, stir-fries. It's kind of a paste form of soy sauce. There are so many kinds but I usually use white.

Peanut butter: For eating by the spoonful.

Ponzu: Almost like a vinaigrette. A super-tangy, kind of sweet and salty sauce made for dipping. I like to make my own mixture but you can buy it bottled.

Red Boat Fish Sauce: If you add just a little bit to a dish, your guests won't be able to put their finger on what exactly is causing the explosive umami sensation in their mouth.

Rue32 Spicy Zaatar Oil: My friend started this company and gave me a jar. Now it doesn't last more than a week in my house. This is an herby, peppery, sesame concoction that tastes good on all types of food but especially Middle Eastern.

Smoked soy sauce: As if soy sauce wasn't addictive enough. This smoked version makes it hard to go back to the OG.

Tahini: Roasted sesame paste that is so silky and toasty I could use it as a moisturizer.

Toasted sesame oil: The perfect finishing touch for any Asian-inspired dish. Essential for salad dressings, ceviche, and dipping sauces.

Tuna: Get the good stuff in the jar with olive oil, or delicious smoked salty tinned tuna from Fishwife. Even better if it's from Portugal, especially the kind with the little chilis in it.

Vinegar: You're going to need to make a little pantry space to stock with vinegar. It's so important for salads, sauces, salsas, pickling, and just adding that little sour kick in the back of your cheeks. Start with apple cider vinegar, balsamic vinegar, white vinegar, red wine vinegar, sherry vinegar, rice vinegar, and white wine vinegar. These are the ones you'll be using all the time. Once you get a little more confident, you can add some other ones. I love sweet potato vinegar and Noma Projects Wild Rose Vinegar.

Dry Ingredients
These need no explanation. Just buy them.

All-purpose flour

Basmati rice

Caramelo tortillas

Cornstarch

Dashi (I like to use the packets because they are so easy.)

Dry breadcrumbs

Ella's Flats crackers

Finn Crisp

Kettl Tea (I don't drink coffee so I like keeping all kinds of delicious teas around for after dinner. Kettl soba cha is my favorite.)

Nuts and seeds: almonds, hazelnuts, pistachios, walnuts, pecans, sesame seeds

Panko breadcrumbs

Pasta, dried (All pasta is good but my favorites are calamarata, mafaldine, rigatoni, linguine, and spaghetti.)

Papa Steve's bars

Short-grain rice (Shirakiku, Koshihikari)

Sourdough bread

Udon noodles

Dairy/Fridge
Keep these things in your fridge and you'll always be able to put a meal together last minute. You'll also always have something ready for a little snack.

Caviar: I've always liked caviar but recently I've become fully obsessed. Any time it's around I have to put it on whatever I'm eating. My favorite way to consume it is with potato chips, crème fraîche, and chives. It's all expensive, there's no getting around it. So save it for a special occasion. I like to order mine from Regalis, Petrossian, or Russ & Daughters—all of these purveyors ship nationwide.

Cheese: Cheddar, gouda, feta, mimolette, provolone, and parmesan are always in my fridge. See my picnic section for more suggestions.

Crème fraîche: Fancy sour cream I keep around for serving with caviar.

Eggs: Look for anything organic, free range, or pasture raised. Happy Egg is one of my favorite brands. The more orange the yoke, the better it is. You want it to look radioactive.

Fresh herbs: Basil, dill, chives, parsley, cilantro, scallions. It's also a great way to start your own little garden, even if you just have a window box. Then you will always have fresh herbs on hand.

Labneh: Tangy Middle Eastern spreadable cheese made from strained yogurt. Use it in a dip, as a spread, or put a little fruit and honey on it for breakfast.

Sour cream: I go through a gallon of sour cream a month. My go-to for making things creamy.

Yogurt: I like strained Greek yogurt for dips and use it in place of sour cream when I'm trying to be healthy.

TOOLS

These tools will make your life easier. Get 'em and thank me later.

Must Haves

Air fryer: When I'm not making dinners for people, I'm using the air fryer to cook a chicken breast and broccoli. It's the best thing for when you just need a healthy meal for yourself or to free up the oven. I love my Philips Premium Airfryer but the Cosori Pro is a good budget pick.

Bowls: Have a big stack of stainless-steel mixing bowls for mixing, marinating, and tossing salads.

Box grater: You'll need this for hand-grating all twelve pounds of cheese in my Mac n' Cheese recipe.

Citrus Squeezer: Squeeze every last drop of juice out of your lemons and limes while straining the seeds.

Colander: If you are making pasta, you need a colander. Also great for rinsing veggies and fruits.

Fish spatula: Flexible and long, it's great for . . . fish . . . but also for squishing things down (like latkes) or turning over anything delicate.

Food processor: You need a food processor, there is no way around it. From shredding potatoes for latkes to chopping nuts in seconds, a food processor will save you so much time.

Kitchen shears: Buy a good pair of heavy-duty scissors that are for the kitchen and nowhere else.

Knives: You don't need a whole expensive knife block. It's better to invest in one or two good knives that you'll have forever if you take good care of them. I buy my knives from Japanese Knife Imports, but other great brands are Wüsthof, Shun, and Henckels. If you only buy one knife, make it a flat-edged santoku knife. A 7- to 9-inch chef's knife and a paring knife are also pretty essential.

Mesh sieve: The key to straining everything. Get one that is big enough to fit over a medium bowl.

Microplane: This is a special grater for garlic cloves, ginger, and citrus, and for creating fluffy clouds of parmesan cheese.

Parchment paper: I get the precut sheets instead of the rolls because they fit the pan perfectly and lay flat. You'll use this stuff all the time to keep things from sticking to pans, and even as a way to cook things.

Pastry brush: Have a couple of these. One for egg washes and baking and one for brushing meats, etc.

Pots and pans: It's easiest to get yourself started with a set. Clad stainless steel is the best bet for durability. All-Clad is the highest quality and will last way longer than you will, but it's pricey so maybe save this one for your wedding registry. Cuisinart is another good brand. If you are worried about sticking, get a couple of good nonstick pans, like the Zwilling Madura or the Frök, but nonstick coating doesn't last forever. It's also great to have a cast-iron skillet. I love Matty Matheson's 10-inch Cast Iron Pan for frying.

Rice cooker: Making rice seems easy, but it's not. Invest in a rice cooker and you'll have perfect rice every time with minimal effort.

Salad spinner: Salad spinners make quick work of washing and drying lettuce, greens, and herbs. If you're taking the time to make a salad, you need to take the time to properly clean everything—and dressing won't stick to wet leaves. I love the one from OXO.

Sheet pans: Get a few of these, or at least more than one. You're going to use these for so many things in this book. Make sure to get the ones that are rimmed, not the flat-style cookie sheets.

Spider: Weird name for this little wire strainer. Great for frying and straining.

Stand mixer or hand mixer: If you plan on doing a lot of baking, invest in a stand mixer. If you're not sure yet, a hand mixer is a less expensive option that takes up a lot less space.

Storage containers: Get a good set of BPA-free storage containers for meal prep and leftovers. Maybe get two sets because friends will definitely want to take leftovers home and then never return your containers.

Thermometer: It sounds scary, but if you have a thermometer, you no longer have to guess about doneness. A candy thermometer is specifically designed to be set on the inside of a pot and it will measure the temperature of liquid sugar for candy-making. You'll need one of those a few times in this book for caramel and meringue. Instant-read thermometers are designed to probe meats or baked goods for an internal temperature reading.

Vitamix blender: This is an expensive one, but if you're really into cooking, there is no comparison. You'll use it all the time and wonder how you ever lived without it.

Ninja also makes a high-speed blender at a lower price point.

Not Required but Will Make Your Life Better

Big Green Egg: The Big Green Egg is a ceramic grill for BBQ that holds in heat far longer than any other grill on the market. It also gives it this signature taste that's almost unexplainable.

Deep fryer: I fry enough that a deep fryer comes in handy. It's better for bigger batches and so much less mess to clean up. I use a T-fal.

Donabe: This Japanese ceramic cooking pot is beautiful to look at while sitting on top of your stove, but you'll use it a lot if you like making healthy steamed vegetables and soups. You can find beautiful donabes at Toiro.

Flat-top grill: I love cooking burgers and meats on my flat-top outside, but also breakfast stuff like hashbrowns. You can get an indoor version too like an electric griddle or just a reversible grill pan.

Gozney Home Pizza Oven: If you love making pizza, this is a great investment. You'll use it all the time, and people will have so much fun coming over to make their own pizzas. It's also great for breads like the Laffa Bread with Michael Solomonov on page 84.

Ice cream maker: This one takes up a lot of cabinet space, but it's worth buying just so you can make Halva Ice Cream with Adeena Sussman on page 91.

LOMI composter: Do your part for Mother Earth and compost. I love making dirt with my LOMI almost more than I like making food. Seriously, I can't stop. This thing is insane—you put all your food scraps in it and dirt for your garden comes out in a few hours. I almost called this book *How to Make Dirt.* Also, in general, try to use environmentally friendly products when you can, from your dishwasher soap all the way down to your cling wrap. Recycle after your guests leave. It's really not that hard. If you use Styrofoam you're an asshole.

Smashula: To make smash burgers, obviously.

Traeger smoker: If you love a big drippy meaty brisket, or a succulent smoky steak, invest in a Traeger. It makes smoking so easy. You'll use it for everything, even peppers.

music ... the only section i'm actually qualified to talk about

My agent Sarah told me she would kill me if I didn't make a playlist for my book. I get really embarrassed when I have to talk about music for some reason, but I guess we're all facing our fears with this book. Scan this QR code and it will take you to a DSP that will lace you with the right music for any type of party.

a little help from my friends

WEED

I love smoking weed with my friends. I love smoking weed when I eat. But my favorite thing in the world is when I'm smoking weed with my friends while eating. Most of my friends smoke weed. Some more than others. But when I was thinking of who to ask to help craft this Weed Guide 101, it was Ben Sinclair's name that was beeping in my head like a fire alarm that's running out of batteries. For those of you who don't know Ben Sinclair, he is the ultimate pothead—so much so that he wrote, directed, and starred in his own show on HBO called *High Maintenance* about a dealer in New York. But really, the show is about weed being a vehicle for human connection, which is why I thought he was

the right one to talk to about all of this. Without further ado, Ben will curate your perfect weed experience.

You know you're at one of benny's parties before you even arrive because (a) there's a casually dressed armed security guard waiting outside, aka The Cowboy, who quickly but fairly appraises your trustworthiness and then inserts an RFID chip into your ass cheek via syringe and (b) the smoke of top-shelf weed enters your nostrils, taking you back to the first time you ever got high.

But before you walk in, you usually catch a glimpse of your own tired reflection in the window and remind yourself that you aren't a loser and that no one at the party is even thinking about you at all. And then you remember the trick that benny taught you, that Beyoncé taught him, where you smile widely and say to yourself in the calm, bright tone of a smooth operator: "Ready!"

Once you walk in, representatives of every living generation mill about, punctuating their sentences with potato chips dripping in $900/oz caviar. A joint the thickness of André the Giant's pinky, affectionately called a "doinker," gets passed to you and you're told it's "the best weed in the world"—the man who grows it is a genius and he's sitting in the corner, rolling a blunt that contains an entire ounce of weed. You notice the doinker's filter is a piece of uncooked fusilli, and you must admit that is genius. You bring the doinker to your lips, forsaking your New Year's resolution to "cool it on the weed," and slurp the terps of indeed the best weed you've ever tasted.

After that, it's all a blur. But you don't get too out of line because The Cowboy is watching . . .

Here are three tips to keeping it classy while you're stoned:

1. If you have cold sores, request your own "sovereign doinker"—there's plenty to go around!
2. As hard as it may be, avoid asking other guests about their net worth.
3. If you think you're too high, think about all the poor souls who can't get high at all, and how lucky you are to even be high in the first place.

Another good friend also happens to be a weed wizard. He even looks like a wizard. His name is Skelly and he owns a company called 710 Labs. He rolls world-famous baseball-bat-size blunts at my parties and everywhere he goes, so I asked him for a dreamy statement about blunts.

The blunt wants a kiss, so you gently press your lips to it. You salivate. You are feeling relaxed and engulfed in the intimacy of its ritual. Laughing and looking at the person on your left who came before you, seeing their glazed eyes, and looking to your right and seeing who is about to be the next initiate.

A flavorful experience with the herb can leave just as much of a lasting impact as a great meal, but marrying the herb with a great meal is a timeless classic humans have enjoyed for ten thousand years. The plentiful bounty our host prepared and presented to you has left you at a loss for words. The blunt comes around one more time, and as some guests snap photos and others yell "This looks delicious," you prepare your plate and give thanks for this bounty and the relaxed reflective state of mind you are in, where you can dive deep into the enjoyment of every bite and get that extra laugh out of your friends' enjoyment as well.

WINE + COCKTAILS

One time I walked into my friend Eric André's house after he had spent all day doing therapy work with MDMA. We were supposed to go out that night and he was nowhere to be found. His house is like a jungle—you have to explore to find him. I was calling his name and when I finally approached his living room I found a trail of 150 empty whip-its that led to

Eric sitting with a hot buttered rum in one hand, a chicken soup in the other hand, a plate of old Erewhon food that looked like squirrels had gotten into it on his lap, and somehow he was also chugging an espresso. He looked up and muttered something along the lines of, "You want to try the best cocktail I've been working on?" He then proceeded to whip me up the most delicious cocktail I've ever had. The recipe is below. The rest of the night was a blur that consisted of a half-naked Justin Bieber singing Sean Kingston's "Beautiful Girls" in the bathroom of Odell Beckham's birthday party, playing the *Seinfeld* theme song at the pinnacle of my DJ set at USC's tailgate, then being kicked out of a Korean restaurant four times before 6 a.m. when we were allowed to eat, which ended in a crowd-participating standing ovation. Anyway, I think the cocktail we had may have had egg whites in it. Here is what Eric has to say about making drinks.

When benny asked me to write a paragraph in his new book about cocktails . . . I was drunk. It was 9:30 a.m. on a Tuesday for Christ's sake, and I was late for work. Then later, after wrapping my Honda around a telephone pole, I begged benny for money to write this paragraph, and he paid me in MiamiCoin, a crypto currency worth less than a Salvadoran peso. I guess what I'm trying to say is, when making cocktails, use real lime juice, not that high-fructose corn syrup bullshit.

More serious draft: The right cocktail at a dinner party can set the night off right, break the ice, lighten the mood, and get the party started. A cocktail is all about balance and personal preference. Alcohol is a delicious poison that makes our brutal existence more tolerable. You might as well throw some sugar and ice on top of your choice of ethanol and enjoy the evening festivities. You only yolo once.

Here's a recipe for maybe the drink I was working on that night, but honestly, I can't remember and neither can he:

MILK PUNCH

Tea blend concentrate
Juice blend
Alcohol blend

For the tea blend: Brew a blend of 75 percent black tea—I recommend qimen (a charcoal roast black tea) and amber red (older tree Nepal black tea)—and 25 percent cinnamon. 9g tea per 8 oz water for like 3 minutes.

For the juice blend: 75 percent pineapple juice, 25 percent fresh lemon juice. Lemon oleo if possible.

For the booze blend: 65 percent clear rum, 30 percent aged rum, 5 percent sherry.

Mix all three so it's 50 percent tea, 25 percent juice, 25 percent booze; and then whatever volume you've got, take about 70 percent of that in warm whole-ass cowfat titty milk and clarify. ♥

To clarify: Let sit on the counter for 1 hour. Do not shake, stir, or touch in any way. Make sure the tea goes into the milk, not the other way around.

Line a large, fine-mesh sieve with a coffee filter or paper towel and slowly strain the mixture into a wide 4-quart container. Once completely filtered (about an hour) transfer to a quart jar or pitcher and chill to serve.

Store tightly sealed in the refrigerator for up to 2 months.

WINE

I'm allergic to wine. When I drink it, I turn hot pink and immediately get a headache. I thought it was all wines until a few years ago when I discovered it was only shitty red wine. Then I discovered the world of natural wine and everything changed.

If you live in the LA area like me, you can pick up great wines at Helen's, Wally's, or Domaine . . . Or you could just say fuck it and go to Stir Crazy and get drunk and forget about this book! The Waves and Parcelle Wines are two great online sources for natural wine that will ship anywhere.

I still don't know anything about wine so whenever I have a question I call my friend Emile Haynie. Emile has been a well-known music producer for decades, working with artists like Lana Del Rey, Bruno Mars, Pink, FKA Twigs, and more. But at this point, it feels like drinking wine is his only job. So follow his gospel below.

Having hosted quite a few wine-geek-centric dinners, or just regular dinners where everyone happily guzzles whatever open bottle is closest to them, I can solidly say that there is an art to selecting which bottle to bring to a dinner and an art to deciding what to serve at the dinner you host. Here are some tips to get you started on the right foot.

Let's start with what to bring. Know your crowd. If you're hanging with a bunch of older folks, lay off the experimental natty barnyard bottle and opt for something classic like a good cab. In that same vein, if you're hanging with a bunch of young foodie kids, lay off the warm-ass bottle of deep red that's been in your cabinet longer than you can remember. Actually, get rid of that bottle, period. You can never go wrong with a bottle of low intervention (organically produced but may or may not have a bit of sulfur) juicy red. This is a good way to describe what you're after to your local wine shop. If you're just starting out, stick to France or Italy. Maybe even suggest a pinot noir from Burgundy. Odds are you're going to end up with something tasty and simple that everyone likes.

If you are going to a specific dinner and you know that the host is passionate about their wine, and you're clueless what to bring, simply ask the host what their favorite wine shop is. Go to that shop, explain who your friend is, and ask what they love and buy that. My favorite dinner guests do this move and they always get reinvited. A sure way to not get that next invite to my house is to show up with some shitty last-minute bottle you got at the grocery store that you think looks cool. Now I have this annoying bottle in the mix with my curated selections and I can't even throw it in a cabinet and use it to cook with some other time. If you ask your host, "What can I bring?" and they say, "Nothing, we're covered," they mean it. Don't show up with some weird bottle and a dessert no one needs.

Bring a couple flowers that are already in some kind of vase.

Pro tip: If you're showing up somewhere and you know your host is a snob but you don't have time to research a nice bottle, bring olive oil. Every cook on every level always needs olive oil. Whether it's a fancy bottle or some basic shit to cook with, it will get used and be appreciated.

When hosting my own dinners, a lot of thought goes into the wine lineup. My perfect night is to start with something bubbly. Champagne, pet-nat, etc. Lightly go into crisp whites and rosés. As the food starts to flow and people are getting a little drunk, I move into reds. Starting with light and juicy and ending with the heavy boys (think Piedmont region, southern France, etc.). Adjust all of this according to your food. If you're making whitefish in a butter sauce, go heavier on the white wines. If you're making beef stew or something, you know what to do.

I love to have something for everyone. Some exotic natty bottles for certain friends. Some more classically produced bottles for others. If you're hosting a big party, large format bottles are always fun. Magnums. Jeroboams. You can find massive bottles that are inexpensive and a blast to crack open and a sure way for everyone to partake.

We also need to talk about temperatures. Assuming that most readers aren't serving up some expensive aged bottle, just play it safe and serve everything cold. Including the reds. Put them all in the fridge a few hours before party time and you're good. Keep your bubbles, rosés, orange wines, and whites as cold as possible. Ice buckets go a long way.

Super-light reds I want cold as well. Heavier reds you want slightly chilled. Just take it out of the fridge thirty minutes or an hour before you crack it open and it should be perfect.

If you're passionate about exploring wines, I highly suggest finding your coolest local shop, sticking with them, and developing a relationship. Find a shop that is more curated with an emphasis on natural wines. Hopefully they will have some classics as well. Build a rapport, explain to them what you love. Be honest when you don't like something. Explore different regions. It's an endless world of selections but you will start discovering what you truly love in due time. Or you can just go buy a bottle of tequila and get hammered way faster and save yourself a hell of a lot of time and money.

DECOR AND VIBE

I pride myself on creating the best-looking parties I can. I want my parties to transport my guests out of everyday life. I have nice little napkins in my favorite colors and I like to collect plates. I'm getting more and more into collecting stuff I love that extends my personal style into everything I do. It's like transforming your home into your own restaurant. You know that feeling when you walk into an amazing restaurant and everything is kind of magical if they have done a good job? Doesn't it make the food taste better? It's the best when you're at home because you can have art you love up on the walls.

I'm usually done prepping and try to get everything tightened up and my nice incense lit before guests arrive. Because once they come in, they crowd around the kitchen and I hate when it's a mess. But however hard I try, whenever I go to one of Jess's parties it makes me look like my parties were decorated by a blind toddler. I don't believe in jacks of all trades, but I'm still trying to figure out what Jess isn't good at. I hate her. But I'm stuck with her. *Weeee!* I enlisted her to help me share some of the fundamentals of vibe creation. Also, she worked with Martha Stewart for more than a decade as an editor at her magazine and her go-to food stylist, which is where she learned most of her tricks. Martha, will you please let me take you on a date?

What follows aren't rules to adhere to, but details to pay attention to. It's taken me a lot of time to realize it's not about making everything look perfect, but about making people feel special and taken care of. Think of the things you love about your favorite restaurant, and how that feels different from a regular night at home. Not just the tastes, but all of your senses, because that is what creates a total experience.

Sight

Setting the table: *I love setting the table. It's your opportunity to create your own style of entertaining. You can be playful and make it unique to you and your personal style. Love certain colors, shapes, patterns, and prints? Here's your chance to make things your signature, or you can switch up little details (like the flowers or napkins, or move from the dining table to the coffee table . . . or the patio!) every time to make it feel fresh.*

Plates: *You don't need the most expensive plates, and they don't even all need to match! But having a grown-up set of dishes that you love is a worthwhile investment. CB2 is a great source for clean modern designs. Target has stoneware collections at a lower price point. Etsy and thrift shops have so many fun vintage sets if that's more your style. I have a dishwasher, so I always make sure everything I have is dishwasher safe for easy cleanup. It's a good idea to have a few platters, serving bowls, and nice oven-to-table casserole dishes too.*

Glassware: *Glasses break, and unless you can afford to replace them all the time, I suggest stocking up on a set of Duralex Picardie glass tumblers. They are classic and cheap and very French looking and come in different colors. They are perfect for wine, water, little cocktails, and espresso. Ikea has similar glasses, and CB2 has the Marta line of glassware that is also great. HAY has the cutest selection of colors. I hate using plastic so I think having enough glasses for everyone is important.*

Cutlery: *You can find decent knock-off designs of all the fancy stuff on Amazon. They will get beat up over time, but you can find a solid collection for eight for under $50. I like everything to match, but it doesn't have to. Thrift stores, Etsy, and estate sales are good sources if you have a little more time and a certain vintage aesthetic you're into. This is where you can have some fun mixing and matching.*

Napkins: *This is a big one for me because it's a little touch that makes a huge difference. Buy a set or two of cloth napkins—a little pop of color and texture makes it feel like a real dinner party. Crumpled-up paper towels look amateur. I love linen napkins from SUAY Sew Shop. They have the best colors and patterned napkins from Block Shop Textiles.*

Lighting: *I don't always have candles, but little votives are the safest and easiest way to get ambient lighting directly on the table, and everyone and everything looks better in mood lighting. Even flameless candles get the job done. Wherever you're eating, try to have a dimmer on the switch, or low-watt lightbulb in the fixture. I don't have a lightbulb higher than 4 watts in my entire home—you can't read a book anywhere, but you instantly feel warm and relaxed.*

Flowers: *Flowers are another great way to make even a mid-week meal feel special. I always keep flowers in the house, even when people aren't coming over, just because they make me happy. Even a bunch of grocery store carnations cut to fit a vase makes a difference. But do cut them to fit the vase— don't just stick them in there! Even if it's just a Ball jar—have something on hand to put flowers in. Guests love to bring flowers too. Or if you're a guest at someone else's home, bring some flowers with a bottle of wine.*

Presentation: In culinary school we learned to present food on a variety of shaped platters "for visual appeal." I only like circular and oval platters: I don't think hard corners belong on a table—it feels very eighties to me (not in a good way). Unless it's a carving or cheese board, which is a good idea to have on hand as well. Keep the rims of your plates clean and free of sloppy fingerprints and smeared sauces. Put a little extra effort into plating the food. It goes a long way.

Color

Fresh herbs and lemon wedges brighten up even the brownest dishes.

Sound

Make sure to have a playlist going (see benny's on page 28) and make sure it's playing at the right volume. It shouldn't compete with conversation—I hate having to yell at people across the table—but it should add some energy to the party.

Smell

Presumably your home will be filled with the aroma of simmering sauces and sizzling meats, but get a few candles or some incense for when people walk in the door—at least to keep in the restroom. Japanese incenses are high quality and are usually made without chemicals. They come in a variety of warming earthy scents. Even burning palo santo before guests arrive is a nice touch. I am super sensitive to chemical smells so I don't recommend cheap artificially scented candles. If you want to splurge, Diptique, Byredo, or Flamingo Estate are all great. But basic natural brands like Mrs. Meyer's are also nice.

Feel

Have a comfortable-ish place for everyone to sit, even if it's a pillow on the floor around a coffee table (I'm going to suggest SUAY again for the best floor cushions if you need them). If you're outside in cool weather, make sure you have heat lamps, cozy throw blankets, or extra jackets for friends. If your chairs are uncomfortable, offer some padding. I like to make everything as soft as possible—this goes for napkins and table linens too! Anything you're touching should be soft!

it's a pool party

A few years ago at Coachella, I was in a pool with Lil' Dicky. We were just hanging out, minding our own business, when *bam*, Kendall Jenner and Hailey Bieber walk through the sliding glass doors. Dave gasped for air as if he were taking his last breath. He was so stunned that the words coming out of his mouth were basically gibberish. He turned to me and told me it was his sole mission that day to make Kendall fall in love with him. Hailey and Kendall changed into bikinis and got in the pool. Dave was pulling out some of his funniest material, which naturally included stories about his penis surgeries and awkward sexual encounters. He had the room in stitches for hours. He even got into a football throwing contest with everyone in the pool and threw a football farther than Dan Marino. He was peacocking at the highest level. It felt like it was a sure shot for him, like it was the beginning of Dave's new life. As the girls got out of the pool to dry off, one of their friends looked at Dave and said, "I really think Kendall wants to fuck you." Dave, trying to act calm while jumping out of his skin, said, "R-r-really???" like a little giggling schoolgirl. The friend then turned to Dave and said, "*No! Are you joking?*" She immediately yelled to Kendall from across the pool, in front of everyone, "I just told Dave you wanted to fuck him, and he actually thought I was serious!" Kendall responded, "I love you, but, no."

Dave's world was shattered. So try to put your best foot forward at a pool party. I'm sure Kendall Jenner won't be there, so you'll probably have a better chance with the girl you're talking to.

Speaking of confidence, a lot of people are scared to cook seafood at home. I don't know why, you're not going to catch these crabs or lobsters yourself. I've made this menu pretty idiot-proof. Just buy really good ingredients and do it. If you don't live close to the sea and have access to great fishmongers at the farmer's market or seafood shops, there are really great sources for buying frozen and fresh seafood online. You can even have live lobsters delivered to your door! I like to buy my seafood from Regalis Foods (which ships nationwide), but check out the Lobster Guy.

That being said, this menu is really only for special occasions. If you're on a budget, don't make this meal because you can't skimp on the product. Make sure to get Martin's Potato Rolls for the lobster roll. All the details matter for this one!

If you're having a pool party or a day at the beach, there is no better combination of food. Besides basting all the food in brown butter, you'll want to baste your body in some too so you can get as tan as possible. My mom always said you're not supposed to swim until thirty minutes after you eat, but she's lying, that rule isn't true. Eat six lobster rolls and drink ten bloody marys while you're floating in the pool, until you get burnt to a crisp. Doctor's orders.

CHIPS *and* CAVIAR

SERVES 8 TO 10

The ultimate high-brow low-brow snack, and my absolute favorite way to eat caviar. I could eat the entire thing all by myself! But don't be that person—caviar is meant to be shared!

1 (50g to 125g) tin caviar, such as kaluga, osetra, or California white sturgeon

1 (8-ounce) container crème fraîche

Finely chopped chives, for garnish

3 (5-ounce) bags kettle-cooked potato chips

Prepare a platter by placing the caviar tin in a small bowl of ice—you'll want to keep it extremely cold, especially if you're outdoors in the sun. Add crème fraîche to a little bowl and chives in an even smaller little bowl. You'll want a non-metal spoon for scooping the caviar.

Arrange some pre-made chips on the platter by scooping a bit of crème fraîche, then caviar, and a little sprinkle of chives on top—but let people do their own thing and go crazy!

BLOODY MARYS

MAKES 8 TO 10

Bloody marys are good because it feels like you're eating, but you're drinking. It's kind of like drinking salsa with vodka in it. It's a really strange concept. I don't even get how it works but it does, and it's delicious.

3 cups tomato juice

3 tablespoons prepared horseradish

2 teaspoons Worcestershire sauce

1 tablespoon smoked soy sauce

¼ cup pickled pepper (pepperoncini) brine

2 lemons, juiced

1 teaspoon freshly ground pepper

Hot sauce, such as Tabasco or Crystal, to taste

8 ounces vodka

Celery, lemon wedges, and olives to garnish

In a large pitcher, combine the tomato juice, horseradish, Worcestershire sauce, smoked soy, pickled pepper brine, lemon juice, pepper, and hot sauce. Stir to combine. Let sit for as long as you can bear—overnight is best so the flavors can really marinate. Pour a little vodka into an ice-filled glass then fill with the Bloody mix. Top with celery, lemon wedges, olives—fuck it—throw pickles in there, whole shrimp—whatever you want! The garnishes are my favorite part.

SHRIMP COCKTAIL

SERVES 8 TO 10

So simple yet so satisfying. Really, I just want something to dip in cocktail sauce.

FOR THE COCKTAIL
SAUCE

1 cup ketchup

2½ tablespoons prepared
horseradish

1 teaspoon
Worcestershire sauce

1 tablespoon Tabasco

Lemon juice

Kosher salt

FOR THE SHRIMP

Ice

2 tablespoons kosher salt

2 tablespoons sugar

2 lemons, thinly sliced

3 bay leaves

1 teaspoon black
peppercorns

2 pounds shell-on jumbo
shrimp, deveined

Cocktail Sauce

In a medium bowl, whisk together the ketchup, horseradish, Worcestershire sauce, and Tabasco. Season to taste with lemon juice and kosher salt.

Fill a large bowl with ice and a bit of water to prepare an ice bath and set aside.

Fill a large pot halfway up with water, 2 tablespoons kosher salt, sugar, lemons, bay leaves, and peppercorns.

Bring the liquid to a boil and reduce to a very low simmer. Add the shrimp, and poach until cooked through, about 4 minutes.

Transfer the shrimp to the ice bath and let sit for about 10 minutes. Transfer to paper towels and peel. Pat dry before serving on clean crushed ice with additional lemon wedges. Serve with Cocktail Sauce on the side.

BROILED OYSTERS

MAKES 24

One time in New Orleans I went on an oyster tour. I was fed a charbroiled oyster at a place called Acme, and in that very moment, I understood how someone could be addicted to heroin. Because over the course of six hours, I had sixty-four oysters. Even my ex-girlfriend, who hates oysters, had a few.

1 stick unsalted butter

4 cloves garlic, minced

¼ teaspoon dried oregano

Pinch chili flakes

¼ cup breadcrumbs

Zest of 3 lemons

½ cup olive oil

1 teaspoon salt

1 cup fresh parsley, finely chopped

1 cup grated parmesan cheese, divided

24 oysters

Heat your grill to 500°F or your oven to broil.

In a small saucepan, gently melt the butter. Add the garlic, oregano, and chili flakes.

In a small bowl combine the breadcrumbs, lemon zest, olive oil, salt, parsley and ½ cup parmesan.

The great thing about grilling oysters is that you don't really have to shuck them, which is the hard part about oysters. Just pop the oysters flat side down on the grill and leave them there until they open, about 2 minutes. Once they open up, tear off the flat shell and return to the grill.

Place 1 tablespoon of butter mixture on each oyster. Cook for about 2 minutes, then sprinkle about 2 tablespoons of the breadcrumb mixture on each oyster. Cook for another 2 minutes, until golden brown around the edges. Top with more parmesan.

FAT DADDY CRABCAKES

MAKES 8 TO 12

A lot of people like their crabcakes fried but I prefer them the classic Baltimore way, where they are thick, baked, and the size of a double hockey puck. These cakes are crispy and buttery on the outside and like a pillow on the inside. I can't have it any other way and after you eat this you won't either.

FOR THE CRABCAKES

28 Ritz crackers, hand crushed (about 1 cup)

½ cup mayonnaise

3 tablespoons Old Bay Seasoning

3 tablespoons Worcestershire sauce

¼ cup whole grain mustard

¼ cup dijon mustard

1 bunch parsley, finely chopped

2 pounds (32 ounces) jumbo lump crab meat, picked through to remove any shells

Freshly ground black pepper

1 stick unsalted butter, melted

Lemon wedges for serving

Tartar Sauce

Preheat the oven to 350°F.

In a large bowl mix together the Ritz crackers, mayonnaise, Old Bay, Worcestershire sauce, whole grain mustard, dijon mustard, parsley, and jumbo lump crab meat. Season with pepper to taste. Mix until well combined.

Form the crab mixture into 8 to 12 (4- to 6-ounce) patties, about ½ cup of mixture each. Chill at least 20 minutes, or freeze at this point. Either way it's a good time to make the Tartar Sauce.

Combine all the ingredients for the Tartar Sauce in a bowl and season to taste with salt and pepper (you might not need any!).

Place crabcakes on a parchment-lined sheet pan and brush with melted butter and bake until golden brown, 20 to 25 minutes. Serve with lots of lemon and Tartar Sauce.

1 cup mayonnaise

1 shallot, minced

2 tablespoons chopped capers

½ cup chopped cornichons, plus 1 tablespoon pickle juice

¼ cup herbs (chives, parsley, tarragon), finely chopped

Zest and juice of 1 lemon

1 tablespoon dijon mustard

1 tablespoon whole grain mustard

Kosher salt and freshly ground black pepper

LOSE YOUR MIND LOBSTER ROLLS

MAKES 8

If cooking lobsters feels too scary, just ask the seafood counter, they will usually do it for you. Or you can buy already picked lobster meat if you're feeling really lazy. If you don't have fresh live lobsters available near you, just sad sleepy-looking guys in sketchy-looking tanks, try ordering online—there are many services that ship overnight directly from Maine. You can order picked lobster meat and buns from some, like the Lobster Guy and Luke's Lobster, so all you have to do is toast and slather and fill your belly.

4 (2½-pounds) or
6 (1½-pounds) live
lobsters

½ cup mayonnaise,
plus more for the rolls

Zest and juice from
1 lemon, plus more
wedges for serving

Kosher salt

8 Martin's hot dog buns

4 tablespoons unsalted
butter, plus 1 stick
unsalted butter, cut into
1-inch cubes

Old Bay Seasoning,
for serving

Finely chopped chives,
for serving

Celery salt, for serving

In a large pot lined with a steamer basket, bring 1 inch of water to a boil. Drop the lobsters headfirst into the pot and cover. Reduce heat to a simmer and steam until the shells just turn bright red, 12 to 14 minutes. Let cool.

To get all the meat out, hold the tail in one hand and the body in the other; twist and pull to separate. For the claws and legs, twist and pull where they're attached to the body. Use a mallet or a heavy pan to crack the shells. Pull the tail out with a fork. Once you've gotten all the meat out, chop it into chunks. Mix with the mayonnaise and the zest and juice of 1 lemon. Salt if needed.

Cut off the sides of the hot dog buns so that they have flat exposed sides. Melt 2 tablespoons butter in a cast-iron skillet. Add four rolls and toast until deep golden brown, about 2 minutes per side. Repeat with the remaining 2 tablespoons of butter and rolls.

Melt the remaining stick of butter in a small saucepan over medium heat. Continue to cook, stirring constantly, until deep golden brown, about 11 to 12 minutes. Immediately transfer to a large heatproof bowl.

Swipe each bun with mayonnaise then add a mountain of lobster meat. Top with Old Bay, chives, and celery salt, and drown in the warm brown butter to serve.

KEY LIME PIE

SERVES 8 TO 10

Jess and I have tasted so many different key lime pies. She's always saying they left the key limes out for too long and it's bitter. I could never tell the difference until we developed ours, and I hate to say it but she's right. Use freshly squeezed lime juice and use it right away.

12 graham crackers

1 stick (8 tablespoons) unsalted butter, melted

3 tablespoons granulated sugar

Kosher salt

2 tablespoons lime zest, finely grated, plus more for serving

4 large egg yolks

1 (14-ounce) can sweetened condensed milk

⅔ cup *freshly squeezed* lime juice from about 6 limes (key limes are even better if you can find them, but you will need a 1-pound bag)

1 cup heavy cream

2 tablespoons confectioners' sugar

Lime zest

Preheat the oven to 350°F.

Pulse the graham crackers in a food processor until finely ground (you should have about 1¾ cups). Add the butter, sugar, and a pinch of salt and pulse until all the crumbs are moistened. Press the crumbs up the side of a 9-inch pie plate. I like to use a spoon or a dry measuring cup to really press in the crust and make it neat, but you can just do it with your fingers and it will be fine. Bake until golden brown and fragrant, about 10 minutes. Remove from the oven and let cool while you make your filling.

Put 2 tablespoons of the lime zest into the bowl of an electric mixer. Add the egg yolks and beat until pale and thick, about 6 minutes. Add condensed milk and beat for about 5 more minutes. Add the lime juice to the bowl. Mix until combined. Pour into the crust and bake until just set, about 10 to 12 minutes.

Let the pie cool completely.

Beat the cream and sugar until soft peaks are formed. Pile on top of the pie and grate more lime zest over the top.

i wish i was an italian grandma

One night my friends Nino and Davide hosted a dinner at my house in LA. Nino's family started an olive oil company called Partanna. Nino brought his father, who seems to live off cheese, bread, and wine but somehow is a tanned man with a six-pack who looks like he's sixteen years old. Italians do things a little differently. Within five minutes there were twenty bottles of wine cracked open and Davide just kept pulling cold cuts, cheeses, and loaves of bread longer than my torso out of some kind of never-ending Willy Wonka–esque paper bag. I felt like we were eating a feast, but then Davide said, "These are just snacks while we cook."

Everyone gathered around my kitchen island and we all took a shot of olive oil so we wouldn't have hangovers. I didn't believe it while we were doing it, but I've done it three times now and it works. So even if you don't eat Italian food and just like to drink, this nugget of information might save your life. As the night went on, spices were thrown into the air, zucchini flowers were stuffed, chicken cutlets were fried to golden perfection, and mountains of parmesan were grated. It was then that I realized how easy it is to fall head over heels for an Italian man. That's amore!

I know that didn't have much to do with the recipes that follow, but, allora! And if you don't know what allora means, it kind of means everything and nothing all at once. Grazie mille.

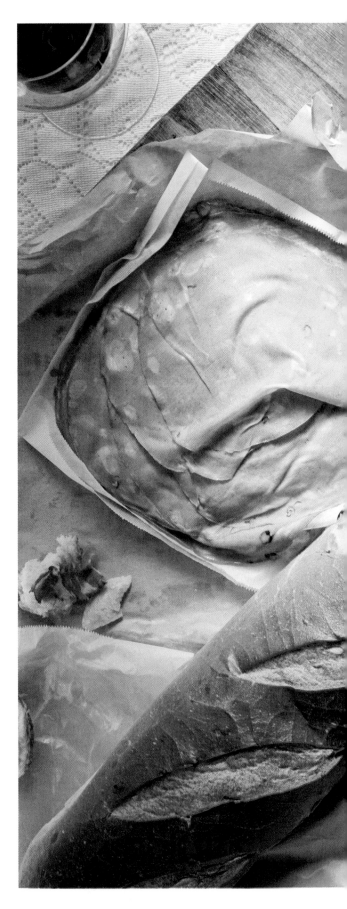

GARLIC BREAD

MAKES 1 LOAF

It's garlic bread; what else do you need to know?

1 head garlic

Olive oil

1 large baguette or loaf of Italian bread

1 stick unsalted butter

1 teaspoon crushed red chili flakes

1 teaspoon dried oregano

2 teaspoons tomato paste

1 tablespoon Calabrian chili spread (if you like it spicy)

Kosher salt and freshly ground black pepper

½ cup grated parmesan

1 cup shredded mozzarella cheese

Finely chopped parsley and chives, for serving

Preheat the oven to 400°F. Cut off the top quarter of the head of garlic. Drizzle with a bit of oil and wrap in foil. Bake until golden brown and very soft, 40 to 50 minutes. Let cool.

Par-cut the bread into 1-inch thick slices—stopping a little more than halfway through so the slices stay connected to the loaf.

Heat your broiler. Place the baguette cut side up on a foil-lined baking sheet. In a food processor (or in a bowl, you can do this by hand), combine the butter, 1 tablespoon olive oil, chili flakes, oregano, tomato paste, Calabrian chili spread, and salt and pepper. Then squeeze the roasted garlic out of its skin right in there. Process (or just stir really well) until everything is smooth and combined. Spread evenly over cut sides of baguette and sprinkle with parmesan and mozzarella. Bake until golden and slightly crisp, 2 to 3 minutes. Sprinkle with chives and parsley; cut into pieces.

CAPRESE *with* ROASTED PEPPER *and* BURRATA

SERVES 8

If you don't feel like roasting your own peppers, buy the best jarred peppers you can and you'll be able to make this salad in two seconds. Be sure to add the truffle oil. I promise you it's worth it. It's the best dressing I've ever had in my life. You'll want to lick the platter when the salad is gone.

2 red or orange bell peppers, seeded and halved

Olive oil

Kosher salt and freshly ground black pepper

2 teaspoons dijon mustard

¼ cup balsamic vinegar

1 teaspoon honey

2 tablespoons mayonnaise

½ teaspoon truffle oil

1 pint cherry tomatoes, halved

2 (6- to 8-ounce) balls burrata or fresh mozzarella, torn

Fresh basil leaves, for garnish

Preheat your broiler with the rack in the upper third of the oven. Place the peppers, skin side up, on a foil-lined baking sheet. Drizzle with a bit of oil and sprinkle with salt and pepper. Broil until well charred. Place in a bowl and cover with plastic. Let steam for about 10 to 20 minutes until softened and cool enough to handle. Discard the skin by rubbing it with a paper towel. You don't have to remove the skin, but it feels a little bit better to eat if you do. Slice into strips and set aside.

In a small bowl, combine the dijon, balsamic, honey, mayo, and truffle oil. Whisk until well combined. Spread on the bottom of a plate or platter.

Build the salad on top of the dressing, sprinkling the peppers and tomatoes to fill the plate. Nestle the torn burrata into the veggies. Drizzle with a bit of olive oil and season with salt and pepper. Sprinkle with basil leaves.

ORANGES *with* CHILI *and* PISTACHIOS

SERVES 8

This salad is here for Nino's dad. He was so happy when he saw Jess making it the night we had the dinner party because she understood the Italian way of just the pistachios and the oranges. It's all you need.

8 oranges (use a variety of colored oranges such as blood, cara cara, and navel)

Drizzle of good olive oil

1 small shallot, very thinly sliced

1 small Fresno chili or red jalapeño, thinly sliced (or a big pinch of crushed chili flakes)

Flaky salt

¼ cup chopped pistachios

To peel the oranges, use a sharp knife, cut a thin slice off both ends of fruit to reveal the flesh, and stand the fruit upright. Then, following the curve of the fruit, cut downward to remove the orange part (the peel) and white part (the pith). You need to cut all the way down to the fruit! Rotate the fruit as you work, until all of the peel and pith is cut away. Thinly slice the oranges crosswise.

Arrange the orange slices on a plate or platter. I like to layer the colors for a cool ombre effect. Drizzle with your best olive oil. Sprinkle with shallots, chili, flaky salt, and the pistachios.

MEATBALLS

MAKES 28 BIG BOYS

The reason these meatballs are so good is because they have a literal pound of parmesan in them. Jess couldn't stop eating these big boys . . . no one could. We had to pry them out of Jess's hands, and she's lactose intolerant.

FOR THE MARINARA

½ cup olive oil

8 cloves garlic, sliced

8 anchovies

Crushed red pepper flakes or Calabrian chili paste, to taste

Salt and pepper, to taste

2 (28-ounce) cans Jersey Fresh Crushed Tomatoes

You won't believe how easy it is to make your own marinara. In a saucepot, heat up the olive oil over medium. Add the garlic and cook until it starts to get golden and smell amazing. Then add the anchovies and red pepper flakes. Mash them with a wooden spoon and season with a good amount of salt and pepper. Carefully add the tomatoes and bring to a boil. Reduce the heat to a simmer and cook, stirring occasionally, until the sauce has reduced a bit, at least 30 minutes but up to an hour. Taste and add more salt and pepper as needed.

For the meatballs, roast the garlic if you haven't already. Add a stick of butter to a wide deep skillet and melt over medium-high heat. Add the onions, season generously with salt and pepper, and cook, stirring occasionally, until deep brown in places. This generally takes 15 to 20 minutes. If they are getting too dark, lower the heat a bit or add a little water to the pan. The onions should be deeply golden and really really soft. Make sure to cool it all a bit before adding the onions to the meat mixture.

Add the bread to a food processor and pulse until you've got fine little crumbs.

To a large bowl, add the cooled caramelized onion, the roasted garlic, the breadcrumbs, milk, cheese, beef, veal, eggs, and parsley. Mix it all together with your hands. Really get in there. Form the mixture into 3-ounce balls.

6 cloves roasted garlic (see page 63)

1 stick unsalted butter

2 large yellow onions, chopped

Kosher salt and freshly ground black pepper

2 slices white bread (2 cups breadcrumbs)

1 cup milk

1 pound parmesan cheese (4 cups)

2 pounds ground beef (80 percent lean)

1 pound ground veal

2 large eggs, lightly beaten

¼ cup parsley, finely chopped

Neutral oil, for frying

I like my balls big. Chill in the fridge for at least 30 minutes and up to overnight.

Now, I like to deep-fry my balls. I heat my fry oil up to about 450°F in my deep fryer and cook a couple at a time for about 3 to 4 minutes, and then I transfer them to a paper towel–lined plate before adding them to the sauce to finish cooking. But if you don't have a deep fryer, don't worry. It takes a little longer in a skillet, but you can still make them crispy on the outside and tender on the inside.

Heat ½ inch of oil in a large deep skillet, wok, or dutch oven. You're going to have to work in batches, but get that oil heated and carefully add the balls, a few at a time. You'll need to keep rotating them every couple of minutes so they get browned all over.

Transfer the balls to the big pot of sauce and let everything simmer together for about an hour so the flavors meld and the balls get really tender. You should make the time for this—you've come this far, don't just do your thing until you're over it. If you want to make spaghetti and meatballs throw some fucking cooked spaghetti in there too!

CHICKEN CUTLETS *with* HONEY, PEPPERS, *and* PARM

SERVES 8

The night of the Italian feast, while the piles of mortadella were building and then disappearing and shots of olive oil were being taken, Matty was in the corner doing his thing, frying up chicken cutlets, bathing them in butter until they were just right. We were all getting drunk and grabbing things out of the fridge. Someone drizzled honey and sprinkled a bunch of spicy little peppers on top. The chicken was gone in seconds. We ate it with our hands like animals. Forget chicken parm, this is the only chicken you ever need to make again.

8 boneless skinless chicken breasts, pounded thin

1 cup panko

1 cup Italian seasoned dry breadcrumbs (such as Progresso)

½ tablespoon kosher salt

½ tablespoon freshly ground pepper

½ cup grated parmesan cheese, plus extra for grating on top of the cutlets

2 eggs

¼ cup water

1 stick unsalted butter

Olive oil

Honey, for drizzling

½ cup sliced pepperoncini or banana peppers

Flaky salt

If your chicken breasts aren't already pounded, slice them in half, butterflying them open (like the pages of this book) into two pieces. Arrange them on a cutting board between two pieces of plastic wrap and pound them thin and evenly (about ¼-inch), using whatever heavy thing you have (meat mallet, cast-iron skillet, a wine bottle).

In a large shallow bowl, pie plate, or cake pan, mix together the panko, dry breadcrumbs, salt, pepper, and parmesan cheese. In another similar bowl or vessel, add the eggs and water, and whisk until well combined.

Keeping one hand dry, use one hand to season the chicken with salt and pepper, and then transfer it to the egg mixture. Make sure it is completely coated with egg, and let the excess drip off for a moment before dunking it into the breadcrumbs. Make sure the chicken is evenly coated with breadcrumbs and set on a plate or a sheet pan. Repeat with all the chicken.

In a large skillet, melt the butter and add a good drizzle of olive oil. Throw a couple of breadcrumbs into the pan and if they sizzle, you're ready to start frying. Add the chicken and adjust the heat so that none of the breadcrumbs or

butter solids burn—keep it at a steady medium. If the butter gets really dark, you might need to carefully transfer it to a heat-safe container to dispose of later, and start fresh for the remaining chicken. Any burnt bits in there will stick to the chicken, and you don't want that to happen. The chicken will take 4 to 5 minutes per side. Transfer to paper towel–lined plates as you go.

To serve, drizzle with a generous drizzle of honey and grate a mountain of parm over the top of the cutlets. Sprinkle with the sliced peppers and a little flaky salt and see if it makes it to the table.

PASTA *with* GREENS, BREADCRUMBS, *and* OLIVES

SERVES 4 TO 6

This pasta is good hot, but it's even better the next day, or for a second dinner, right out of the Tupperware a few hours later. The noodles soak up all the flavor, and it's incredible, even ice cold. This is a great way to get rid of greens that are getting mooshad in the fridge or in the garden.

½ pound wide noodles, such as mafaldine

½ cup olive oil

6 cloves garlic, thinly sliced

5 anchovies

1 teaspoon crushed chili flakes

3 to 4 cups mixed greens (such as Swiss chard, kale, spinach), finely chopped

1 bunch dill, roughly chopped

½ bunch parsley, finely chopped

½ cup basil leaves

1 cup green olives, pitted and roughly chopped

1 cup fresh toasted breadcrumbs

Parmesan cheese, for serving

Boil pasta according to package instructions. Reserve a little bit of pasta water before draining.

Heat a large, deep skillet over medium. Add ½ cup olive oil and sauté garlic until golden brown, about 2 minutes. Add the anchovies and cook until they begin to soften and melt, about 4 minutes. Add chili flakes and cook for another minute. Slowly, start adding the greens and the herbs, and continue cooking in batches until they are all wilted, about 6 to 8 minutes. Add olives and cooked pasta. Mix to combine. Add a little pasta water if the oil isn't clinging to the pasta. Season to taste with salt and pepper. Serve with breadcrumbs and parmesan cheese sprinkled on top.

TIRAMISU

SERVES 12 TO 14

This is basically Italian banana pudding. It's impossible to take just one bite.

6 large egg yolks

1 cup sugar

1 cup heavy cream

15 ounces mascarpone

1⅓ cups freshly brewed espresso or strong cold-brew coffee

¼ cup Kahlua or Tia Maria

Cocoa powder, for dusting

24 ladyfingers

In the bowl of an electric mixer using the whisk attachment, whisk the egg yolks and ½ cup sugar until pale and fluffy (they will expand like three times in size, and this might take a few minutes). Transfer to a large bowl and set aside. Wipe out the mixer bowl.

In the mixer bowl, combine the cream and $\frac{1}{4}$ cup sugar. Whisk until medium-soft peaks form (when you take out the whisk, the tip of the cream should still be kind of floppy, but not too floppy). Add the mascarpone and whisk on medium speed until the mixture is soft and smooth with medium peaks. Gently fold in the egg yolk mixture with a rubber spatula until combined.

Combine the espresso, coffee liquor, and remaining sugar in a medium bowl.

Dust the bottom of a 9x13 baking dish with 2 tablespoons of cocoa powder. Arrange the ladyfingers, sugared side up, to completely cover the bottom, breaking some in half if necessary. The Italian nonnas say not to dip the ladyfingers, but instead use a spoon to carefully soak just the tops of the ladyfingers so they don't get too soggy. This takes longer than dipping them, but it's worth it.

Cover the ladyfingers with half of the mascarpone mixture and repeat the process. Sprinkle the top with 2 tablespoons of cocoa powder and let sit—24 hours is best but make sure that you let it sit for at least 4 hours before serving.

saucy
shawarma
soiree

In 2019, the James Beard Foundation awarded Outstanding Restaurant to the Israeli restaurant Zahav. If you've never heard of Michael Solomonov, it's time to get familiar. When I first heard Michael's story, I was instantly drawn to him because, like my brother, he struggled with addiction. It wasn't easy but he created a culinary empire with twenty-four restaurants and counting. He cooks with passion, soul, and a whole lot of heart. Plus, he has a cute little punim. I can't believe he agreed to craft this menu with me. Selfishly, I don't care if you make these recipes (even though you should), because I'm going to make them every day. And as if things couldn't get any better, Adeena Sussman gave us a recipe for the most mind-blowing dessert I've ever had. Adeena is a recipe developer and cookbook author based in Israel, and she is one of the most talented cooks I know. This is a perfect menu. You have a beautiful plate of meat and French fries that you shove into a laffa bread as soft as a pillow, then you smother it in sauce and salad and then stuff your face.

Do not make this menu without making the sauces. Honestly, you could just make the sauces and lick them off your fingers. But make everything, please.

ZHOUG

MAKES 1 CUP

5 serrano chilis

5 jalapeños

10 cloves garlic

Kosher salt

1 tablespoon ground coriander

½ tablespoon ground ginger

½ tablespoon ground cardamom

1 cup olive oil

Juice of 1 lemon

Combine the chilis and garlic and a bit of salt in the food processor and blend until smooth. Set a fine mesh sieve over a bowl. Cover with a paper towel and let drain for 5 to 7 days. Discard the liquid.

Stir in the coriander, ginger, cardamom, olive oil, lemon juice, and season to taste with salt.

WHITE SAUCE,
page 82

ZHOUG,
page 80

TAHINI,
page 82

WHITE SAUCE

MAKES 1¼ CUPS

½ cup yogurt

¾ cup mayonnaise

3 tablespoons white vinegar

2 tablespoons sugar

1 tablespoon garlic powder

1 teaspoon dried dill

Kosher salt and freshly ground black pepper, to taste

In a medium bowl, combine all the ingredients except the salt and pepper and whisk until smooth. Taste, then season. Store in an airtight container for up to a week.

TAHINI

MAKES ¾ CUPS

½ cup tahini, room temperature

Juice from 1 lemon (3 tablespoons)

1 teaspoon ground cumin

½ teaspoon garlic powder

½ cup water

Kosher salt

In a medium bowl combine the tahini, lemon juice, cumin and garlic powder. Mix to combine. I like to add the water in a little bit at a time while stirring—you might need a little more or a little less depending on the tahini you used. It will seize up a little bit at first, but continue adding a tablespoon at a time to smooth it out. Season to taste with salt.

PICKLY SALAD

SERVES 8

I don't really know what sumac is (after looking it up apparently it comes from a plant) but every time I put it on something it just tastes better. It's like squeezing super-intense lemon over everything, almost like a sour candy. It's the acid you need to tie everything in this meal together.

6 Persian cucumbers, halved and thinly sliced

1 pint cherry tomatoes, halved

½ red onion, thinly sliced

1 bunch mint, stripped from stems

¼ cup white vinegar

2 tablespoons olive oil

Sumac, to taste

Kosher salt and freshly ground black pepper

In a large bowl, toss together the cucumbers, tomatoes, onion, and mint leaves with the vinegar and oil. Season generously with sumac, salt, and pepper. Let sit 5 to 10 minutes before serving. Everything should soften up and almost pickle itself a little bit.

LAFFA BREAD *with* MICHAEL SOLOMONOV

SERVES 8

I like laffa better than pita because you can stuff more into a sandwich. Try to do this in a pizza oven or on a pizza stone if you have one. If you don't, making it in the oven is fine. It will be so much better than anything you can buy in the store. You might want to double the recipe so you have extra for leftovers.

2¼ teaspoons (1 package) active dry yeast

2 teaspoons sugar

2 cups all-purpose flour

2 cups bread flour

1½ teaspoons kosher salt

2 tablespoons olive oil

In a small bowl, mix ½ cup water, yeast, and sugar and let stand until foamy, about 5 minutes.

Combine the all-purpose flour, bread flour, and salt in the bowl of a stand mixer fitted with the dough hook. Mix on low speed until blended. Add the yeast mixture, another ½ cup water, and the oil and mix on low until the dough forms a ball that pulls clear of the sides and bottom of the bowl. (If after a minute the mixture doesn't form a ball, add a tablespoon of water.) The moment the dough starts to pull clear of the bottom of the bowl, add ½ cup water and continue mixing until incorporated. The dough should feel tacky when slapped with a clean hand, but it should not stick. (If it sticks, add more flour, a tablespoon at a time.)

Cover the bowl with the dough with plastic wrap and let rise at room temperature until doubled in size, about an hour. Alternatively, let it rise in the refrigerator overnight.

Preheat the oven to 500°F, with a rack in the upper third. Place a baking stone or an inverted baking sheet in the oven to preheat as well.

Pat the dough down and divide into eight equal portions. Roll the dough into eight balls the size of a baseball. Cover with a cloth and let rise until they are about the size of softballs.

Roll each dough ball as thin as possible (less than ⅛ inch is ideal) with a floured rolling pin on a floured work surface so the laffa is the size of a frisbee. Drape one laffa over your outstretched hand and quickly invert it onto the baking stone or baking sheet, quickly pulling any wrinkles flat. Bake the laffa until puffy and cooked through, about 1 minute. Serve immediately.

MATBUCHA *with* MICHAEL SOLOMONOV

SERVES 8 (MAKES ABOUT 2 CUPS)

There is a zero percent chance you know how to pronounce this dish, so call it whatever you want, but just make it.

2 red bell peppers, cored, seeded, and chopped

2 yellow onions, chopped

6 garlic cloves, sliced

2 tablespoons kosher salt, plus more for seasoning

½ cup canola oil

16 plum tomatoes, quartered

Scoop of tomato paste (if needed)

Lemon, juiced

Olive oil, for drizzling

Cilantro leaves, for serving

In a straight-sided skillet or sauce pot over medium-high heat, sauté the peppers, onions, and garlic with kosher salt and canola oil. When the vegetables are translucent, about 15 minutes, add the tomatoes. Cook for 1 to 1½ hours, or until the mixture resembles a chunky tomato sauce. This can take a little longer if your tomatoes are out of season and rock hard—don't rush it. If it's been longer than 2 hours and nothing is happening, add a little tomato paste for extra flavor and a little more water to get things moving, but you want the mixture to be deep red and pasty. Transfer to a bowl, taste, and add salt, a squeeze of lemon juice, and a drizzle of olive oil. Scatter cilantro leaves on top. If making ahead of time, bring back to room temperature before serving.

FRENCH FRIES

SERVES 8

I know this preparation seems complicated and ridiculous, but I promise this will be the most insane fry you've ever had.

6 russet potatoes, cut into ½-inch wedges

¼ cup apple cider vinegar

½ cup beef tallow, for frying

1 quart neutral oil, for frying

Kosher salt, for seasoning

Add the cut potatoes to the biggest bowl you have and cover with water. Add the apple cider vinegar and let soak in the fridge for at least 2 hours, up to overnight. Drain, and set up a steamer basket inside of a large pot filled with about an inch of water. Add the potatoes and steam until almost tender but not falling apart, about 10 minutes. This par-cooks the potatoes and allows them to get super crispy later on.

Transfer the steamed fries to parchment-lined rimmed baking sheets, and freeze until solid, about an hour (this seals the surface of the fry and guarantees it will be as crispy as possible).

Heat tallow and oil to 400°F. Fry in small batches until golden brown and crispy, about 5 minutes. Season with salt and eat immediately.

LAMB SHAWARMA *with* MICHAEL SOLOMONOV

SERVES 8

This succulent hunk of meat is the real main attraction of this meal. This recipe is so easy, but your friends will think you've been cooking this thing for two weeks. It's a total showstopper. The only problem is that your entire kitchen may become yellowish orange from the turmeric. But who doesn't love an orange explosion? Seriously, your kitchen, hands, and clothes may all be ruined if you're not careful. Be neat and wear an apron.

FOR THE SHAWARMA SPICE

6 tablespoons ground turmeric

3½ tablespoons kosher salt

2½ tablespoons ground cumin

1½ tablespoons allspice

1½ tablespoons garlic powder

4 teaspoons ground fenugreek

2 teaspoons ground black pepper

2 teaspoons cayenne

¾ teaspoon ground cinnamon

2½ tablespoons of the Shawarma Spice

1 tablespoon kosher salt

1 (4-pound) boneless lamb shoulder, butterflied (ask your butcher to do this for you)

2 tablespoons canola oil

For the Shawarma Spice: Combine all ingredients in a small bowl and mix well. Store in the pantry in an airtight container for up to six months.

Mix the Shawarma Spice and salt in a small bowl. Rub this mixture all over the lamb, cover, and refrigerate overnight.

The next day, preheat the oven to 450°F.

Roll up the lamb and tie it together with butcher's twine. Put the lamb on a baking sheet or roasting pan and roast for 30 minutes, then reduce the heat to 275°F and roast for another 2½ to 3 hours, rotating every 30 minutes, or until a meat thermometer inserted into the center of the lamb registers 160°F. Remove from the oven and let cool to room temperature.

Wrap the lamb tightly in plastic and refrigerate for at least 3 hours (preferably overnight) to make the lamb easier to slice.

To serve the shawarma, unwrap the lamb and slice it against the grain as thinly as you can. Place a cast-iron skillet over medium-high heat and add the oil. Fry the sliced lamb for about 3 minutes, or until it's hot and slightly crispy. Serve on laffa with your favorite sauces, Matbucha, and Pickly Salad.

HALVA ICE CREAM *with* ADEENA SUSSMAN

MAKES 3 CUPS/SERVES 6

This recipe is inspired by the love of tahini that Mike and I share, and the many wonderful things you can do with it. And also by my love for Mike, my favorite chef and one of my favorite people. He honored me by topping the soft-serve at Laser Wolf Brooklyn with my tahini magic shell, so I'm returning the favor here by dedicating my halva-like creation to him. It's important to use coconut cream or at least full-fat coconut milk, but not a sweetened product such as Coco López. Tahini adds richness and slick mouthfeel, and eliminates the need for any eggs, rendering this dessert, like, totally vegan. The roasted sesame seeds and fudgy flecks of medjool date put it over the edge. Unless you've got a compressor-style ice cream maker (baller that you are), make sure to set your ice cream maker bowl in the freezer at least 8 hours in advance.

5 tablespoons sesame seeds

2 cups coconut cream or full-fat coconut milk

1 cup pure tahini, plus more for drizzling

½ cup silan (date syrup) or maple syrup, plus more for drizzling

2 teaspoons vanilla paste or vanilla extract

¼ teaspoon Maldon Sea Salt or kosher salt, plus more for sprinkling

6 large, soft medjool dates, pitted and chopped

Preheat the oven to 375°F. Arrange the sesame seeds on a rimmed baking sheet and roast until fragrant and deep golden, 9 to 10 minutes. Remove from the oven and transfer to a plate to cool. In a large bowl, whisk together the coconut cream, tahini, silan or maple syrup, vanilla, and salt. Transfer to the ice cream maker and process until frozen, adding the cooled sesame seeds and dates during the last 2 minutes of processing (just as the ice cream begins to take shape), 15 to 20 minutes total. To serve immediately, divide the ice cream among bowls, drizzle with silan, and sprinkle with sesame seeds and salt.

my big fat
greek wedding

I ate Greek food so much growing up that if you bit into my arm it would taste like tzatziki. My mom worked in a different state and didn't get home until late, so cheap takeout meals happened regularly. There's something about Greek food that just tastes like it's made with love. I might have my body wrapped in phyllo when I die so all my best friends can take a little bite out of me. What part of your body would you like wrapped in phyllo dough?

The fundamental building blocks of Greek cooking are oregano, lemon, garlic, dill, and olive oil. Doesn't that combo sound perfect? It's the type of food you can eat when you're on a diet, but also the type of food where you can smoke a two-foot-long blunt, sink into a couch, and stuff your face with it until you can't breathe. The rawness of the onion cutting the fat of the shaved meats mixed with the crispness of the peppers and tomatoes smothered in a yogurt sauce makes any human want to squeal with excitement the second it touches their lips.

I've never even been to Greece. I almost went one time for my friend Jessie Ware's wedding but I backed out at the last second because I'm scared of flying. I'm so scared of flying that one time Ed Sheeran and I took a boat from New York City to London. One night we cuddled in the same bed and watched *Titanic* together. It was romantic and we wound up making his biggest album to date. So I guess stuff your face with Greek food for thirty years and let your neuroses overcome you so much that you refuse to fly and become a professional music producer with a cookbook with recipes for food you love from places you are too afraid to visit.

TZATZIKI

MAKES 1 PINT

Food is primarily a vehicle for dip for me. Sometimes I find myself putting my entire fist into a bowl of tzatziki and licking it off. You decide what your vehicle will be. Pita bread works too. Tzatziki is creamy, tangy, and full of fresh dill. It's cooling, refreshing, and everything you need to tie the flavors of a gyro together.

1 medium cucumber

Kosher salt

1 garlic clove

1 lemon

1 cup full-fat Greek yogurt

1 cup sour cream

⅓ cup olive oil

¼ cup dill, chopped

Set a fine mesh sieve over a medium bowl. Grate the cucumber on the large holes of a box grater and transfer to the sieve. Sprinkle with a generous amount of kosher salt, cover with plastic wrap, and let sit in the refrigerator overnight.

Give the cucumbers one extra squeeze with your hands while they are in the sieve to get out any remaining liquid before transferring to a fresh bowl. Grate the garlic clove and zest the lemon into the bowl, then add the juice from half of the lemon. Stir in the yogurt, sour cream, olive oil, and dill. Season to taste with salt and extra lemon juice if necessary.

GREEK SALAD

SERVES 8

If you've had a Greek salad, you probably had it the wrong way. It's a menu item most people stay away from because more often than not it's watery and soggy with tomatoes that are rock hard and orange. Here is the right way to make it. Don't ever go back. Please!!!

1 lemon

2 tablespoons red wine vinegar

¼ cup Greek olive oil

¼ teaspoon dried oregano

Kosher salt

Freshly ground black pepper

8 medium tomatoes, cut into wedges

½ green pepper, diced

½ red onion, thinly sliced

8 ounces feta cheese, cut into large cubes

In a large bowl, whisk together the juice from the lemon, red wine vinegar, olive oil, and dried oregano. Season to taste with salt and pepper. Add the tomatoes, pepper, onion, and feta. Toss to combine and add more salt, pepper, and oregano to taste.

SPANAKOPITA TRIANGLES

MAKES 30 TRIANGLES

When I was a kid, my mom always had a frozen package of spanakopita triangles from Trader Joe's. I have a soft spot for them in my heart even though they were so frostbitten they looked more like large ice cubes than spanakopita. Even if you think you hate spinach, I promise the combination of the feta cheese and flaky buttery phyllo dough will turn you into a believer. When we tested this recipe, I added flaky salt to the top of the dough after I baked it, but I remember Cashmere Cat saying how salty it was, so use your Salt Bae arm sparingly.

2 tablespoons unsalted butter, plus 1 stick for brushing

1 red onion, finely chopped

1 clove garlic, finely chopped

2 pounds (32 ounces) spinach (baby is fine)

Kosher salt

Freshly ground black pepper

3 scallions, thinly sliced

8 ounces feta cheese, crumbled

2 large eggs, beaten

1 handful dill, chopped

1 lemon

20 sheets phyllo dough (look for this in the freezer section of your grocery store)

Extra virgin olive oil

Place a large pan with deep sides over medium-high heat. Melt 2 tablespoons butter. Sauté the onion until soft and translucent, about 8 minutes. Add the garlic and cook until fragrant, about 2 minutes more. Start adding the spinach in batches and cook until wilted, about 2 minutes. It just needs to be floppy and bright green—you don't need to go crazy. Season with salt and pepper to taste and transfer to a bowl to cool.

Once cool enough to handle, transfer the mixture to a fine mesh sieve and, using your hands, press hard to squeeze out all the liquid. You can even spread it out on a few paper towels to absorb any extra moisture. You want the spanakopita to be super crispy, so make sure you try to get *alllll* the liquid out.

Wipe out any liquid from the bowl you used to cool the spinach and put the mixture back in that bowl. Mix in the scallions, feta, eggs, dill, the zest of the lemon, and a bit of the juice. Taste to see if it needs a bit more. Season with salt and pepper to taste.

Preheat the oven to 375°F.

In a small pot on the stovetop, over medium heat (or in a microwave-safe bowl in the microwave), melt the remaining stick of butter.

Make sure you keep the phyllo covered with a damp paper towel while you work or it will get dry and brittle.

Start with one sheet of phyllo dough. Set it on a large cutting board and brush it with a bit of melted butter. Cover with another sheet. Cut each piece into 3 (4-inch) strips the long way. Add 2 tablespoons of the spinach filling to one side of each strip. Fold one corner over the filling to make a triangle and continue folding the triangle over itself until you have used the whole strip of dough. Brush with more butter.

Brush the bottom of two rimmed baking sheets with olive oil and place the triangles on top. Brush the triangles with more butter. Bake until golden and crispy, about 20 to 25 minutes.

These are great to make ahead of time. You can freeze them on the sheet tray and then transfer to a freezer bag, and they are ready to bake any time! To bake from frozen follow the same instructions as above but cook for about 35 minutes, or until deeply golden brown.

GYRO

SERVES 6 TO 8

When my mom and I went to our favorite Greek restaurant Reston Kabob, we would get a gyro plate and get four full meals out of it. I still dream of that place. Before I move on, how the fuck do you pronounce gyro? Is it YER-O? or is it JI-RO? They used a white sauce like the one on page 82, so you might want to make a batch of that along with the tzatziki. Matty Matheson showed me this technique to make the easiest gyro meat ever at home. You cook it in a loaf pan instead of a huge standing spit-rotisserie. It saves so much time and honestly tastes close enough to the rotisserie kind that none of your guests will notice. I like to assemble these sandwiches one by one and hand them out to my friends and watch their minds be blown! This way you can ask everyone what toppings they like and they can eat it right away instead of letting it sit on a platter for too long.

1 pound ground beef

1 pound ground lamb

1 tablespoon ground coriander

2 tablespoons garlic powder

2 teaspoons ground oregano

2 teaspoons ground thyme

1 teaspoon cayenne pepper

1 tablespoon ground black pepper

1 tablespoon kosher salt

8 pita

Tzatziki (recipe page 95)

White Sauce (recipe page 82)

Greek Salad (recipe page 96)

Preheat the oven to 375°F.

Line a 9x5-inch loaf pan with parchment paper.

Place the ground meat and spices in an electric mixer fit with the paddle attachment. Mix on low for 30 seconds. Increase the speed gradually and mix on medium-high until the meat is even and smooth, about 1 minute.

Firmly pack the meat into the loaf pan. Gently bang the pan against the counter to get rid of air pockets.

Place the loaf pan in a casserole dish halfway filled with water to create a bain-marie.

Place the prepared bain-marie on the middle rack of the oven and bake until internal temperature reaches 150°F, about 1 hour 20 minutes.

Remove the meatloaf from the oven. Carefully remove the meat from the loaf pan and let rest for a minimum of 10 minutes. Thinly slice the meat and place on a pita topped with Tzatziki, White Sauce, and Greek Salad.

BAKLAVA

MAKES 36

I love pistachios so much. Pistachios and the combination of flaky phyllo dough and honey turns me into a sweet sticky boi.

3 cups toasted walnut halves

1 cup pistachios, shelled and roasted, plus ¼ cup finely ground

2 teaspoons ground cinnamon

1¾ cups sugar

Pinch of salt

1 lemon, zested

1 teaspoon vanilla extract

½ cup honey

3 sticks unsalted butter, melted and cooled

28 sheets phyllo dough

Preheat the oven to 375°F.

In a food processor, pulse the walnuts, 1 cup pistachios, cinnamon, ½ cup sugar, and a pinch of salt until finely ground. If you don't have a food processor, chop the nuts by hand or put them in a ziplock bag and crush them with a pan.

In a medium saucepan, combine 1 cup water, 1¼ cups sugar, and the zest of 1 lemon and heat over medium-high heat. Bring to a boil, then reduce the heat to a low simmer and stir until the sugar has dissolved, about 2 minutes. Remove from the heat and stir in the vanilla and honey until combined. Let cool while the baklava bakes.

Brush a 9x13-inch baking pan with butter. Carefully layer 7 phyllo sheets into the pan, brushing butter between each layer as you build. Sprinkle a third of the nut mixture over the top. Repeat two more times, then place 7 more phyllo sheets on top of the last layer of nut mixture, brushing butter between each layer.

Brush the top layer with a lot of butter (½ cup). Cut the baklava lengthwise three times to create four equal strips. Then make diagonal cuts at a 45-degree angle about nine times, to create thirty-six diamond-shaped pieces.

Bake until deep golden brown, about 35 minutes. Remove from the oven and carefully pour the syrup over the baklava. Sprinkle with pistachio dust and let cool before serving.

artsy
fartsy

My favorite family to have dinner with is Jonas Wood and Shio Kusaka. Their kids, Kiki and Momo, are cooler than any adult friends I have. We have the best conversations about art, music, and life, and I always leave with beautiful advice from an eleven-year-old. Jonas and Shio are incredible artists, so it's no surprise that their children are extremely talented as well. So much so that they drew me and had plates made of my face. My friends think they made me look like a gremlin, but I think they are cute. Shio is Japanese and very health conscious, so we always eat delicious healthy food.

This is a typical meal for us. I added some tempura, because why not? Nobody is angry when a plate of tempura is put on the table. It's important to get sashimi-grade fish when you're making this menu, or I think you can actually die. Please don't die. Have fun, kids.

WATERMELON SHISO SLUSHIE

SERVES 8

1 medium seedless watermelon (6 pounds), rinds removed, cut into chunks

½ cup sugar

10 shiso leaves

4 cups ice

1 (360-mL) bottle dry sake

Who doesn't love shiso? Who doesn't love watermelon? Who doesn't love a slushie?

Add all ingredients to the blender. Blend and enjoy.

TEMPURA MUSHROOMS

SERVES 8

Tempura is undefeated. It's light and crispy at the same time. It doesn't even matter what you put inside. Honestly, if you gave me poop tempura there's a good chance I'd eat it as long as there's a nice sauce next to it.

Neutral oil, for frying

1½ cups all-purpose flour

1 cup cornstarch

3 cups ice cold sparkling water

2 pounds mixed wild mushrooms, such as oyster, enoki, and maitake, torn into 2-inch pieces

Kosher salt

½ cup dashi

2 tablespoons mirin

2 tablespoon soy sauce

In a large deep skillet or dutch oven, preheat about 2 inches of oil to 350°F.

In a large bowl, whisk together the flour, cornstarch, and sparkling water. Like pancake batter, you don't want to overmix. A few lumps are better than it being too smooth and overmixed.

Holding the stem ends of the mushrooms, dip the clusters into the batter and allow any excess batter to drip off. Carefully lower the clusters, about four at a time, into the oil and cook until really crispy and golden brown, about 4 minutes.

Transfer the mushrooms to paper towel–lined plates and sprinkle with a generous amount of salt. Bonus points for flavored salt here, like yuzu, matcha, or seaweed.

Make the sauce: combine the dashi, mirin, and soy sauce.

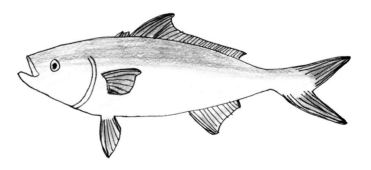

GOMAE

SERVES 8

Gomae is such a good side or snack. It somehow feels like you're eating unhealthy even though it's healthy. I make it in huge batches so it's always around.

2 pounds spinach

Salt for blanching

½ cup + ¼ cup toasted sesame seeds

3 tablespoons good soy sauce

2 tablespoons mirin

2 tablespoons sake

2 tablespoons light brown sugar

Make sure your spinach is clean.

Bring a large pot of salted water to a boil. Prepare an ice bath. Add the spinach to the boiling water and cook for a minute or two, until it's bright green. Transfer the spinach to the ice bath. Let cool completely and then dry off completely. I like to squeeze it in a clean kitchen towel, but you can just squeeze it in your hands and then spread out on paper towels too.

Using a big mortar and pestle (or a food processer) crush ½ cup of sesame seeds until they are mostly smooth but have a little texture left, and transfer them to a large bowl. Then crush the remaining seeds until they are completely smooth. Stir in soy sauce, mirin, sake, and sugar. Mix in the spinach and serve.

SUSHI BATHTUB BOWL (CHIRASHI)

MAKES 8

My friend Chloe calls this dish the bathtub because I have a tub that looks very much like a bento box. This recipe is the one thing I taught all my friends how to make during the pandemic (shout-out to Eric from Sushi Zo for the OG recipe). One of my friends cooks it for every date he has, but then he's scared for the second date because he doesn't know how to cook anything else. So I hope this book helps you, Jake.

If you want to make your own ponzu like I do, add 100 mL mirin to a pot and allow the alcohol to burn off by boiling for a minute or two. Combine with 120 mL soy sauce, 100 mL yuzu juice, and 50 mL Japanese rice vinegar. Add 10g kombu and store in the fridge.

2 cups short-grain white rice

Rice vinegar, to taste

6 sashimi-grade scallops cut into ½-inch pieces

¼ cup Kewpie mayo

Big pinch togarashi

Big pinch kosher salt

Drizzle of sesame oil, for serving

Drizzle of ponzu, for serving

Drizzle of soy sauce, for serving

Pickled ginger, chopped, for serving

Pickled daikon, sliced, for serving

Shiso leaves, for serving

Furikake, for serving

To prepare the sushi rice, soak the rice in cold water in the rice cooker insert for 1 to 2 hours. Drain the rice. Push your pinky finger into the rice, and fill the insert with cold water, just up to the indentation your finger made. Then cook the rice in the rice cooker. It should take about 1 hour. Once cooked, add a bit of rice vinegar to taste.

In a small bowl, combine the scallops, mayo, togarashi, and salt. Mix together.

To create the bowl, start with a bed of rice. Add the scallop mixture and drizzle with the sesame oil, ponzu, and a little soy sauce. Arrange some pickled ginger and daikon then sprinkle with shiso leaves and a bit of furikake.

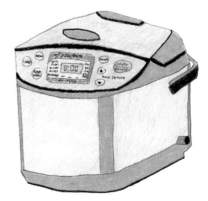

MISO CARAMEL THUMBPRINT COOKIE

MAKES 32 COOKIES

Jess made a sweet potato bread with a miso tahini butter for her book Health Nut *that put me into a state of bliss I didn't think was possible. I asked her for the recipe and she said it was for her own cookbook, so this is the closest I could get. And since you've never had the bread (yet), this will make you pretty happy.*

1¼ cups all-purpose flour

½ teaspoon baking powder

½ teaspoon kosher salt

1 stick unsalted butter, room temperature, plus 1 tablespoon

¾ cups tahini

⅓ cup light brown sugar

½ cup granulated sugar

1 large egg

1 teaspoon vanilla extract or paste

2 tablespoons sesame seeds, toasted

½ cup maple syrup

2 tablespoons heavy cream

2 tablespoons white miso

Preheat the oven to 350°F.

Whisk together the all-purpose flour, baking powder, and salt until combined.

In the bowl of an electric stand mixer fitted with the paddle attachment, combine the stick of butter and tahini. Beat on medium-high speed until light and fluffy, about 6 minutes. Add the sugars and beat until light and fluffy again. Add the egg and scrape down the sides of the bowl. Add the vanilla. Reduce mixer to low speed and add flour mixture. Mix just to combine.

Line two rimmed baking sheets with parchment paper. Roll a tablespoon of the dough into balls and then roll in the sesame seeds. Arrange the balls on sheet trays 1 inch apart. Bake for 10 minutes. Remove from the oven and make an indentation in the center of each cookie. Return to the oven and bake until golden brown, about 6 minutes more.

To make the caramel, add the maple syrup to a medium saucepan. Heat over medium-high heat until the temperature reaches 230°F. Remove from the heat and stir in the remaining butter, heavy cream, and miso. Let cool a bit before spooning a teaspoon of filling into the center of the cookies. Let firm up in the fridge for about 20 minutes before serving.

take me to the
cheesy rodeo

A lot of people don't know this, but I was born in Texas. Even though I moved when I was a year old, I've got a soft spot for this menu because it's in my blood. Tex-Mex is the easiest entry point to Mexican food for a not-so-adventurous eater. It's kind of like Mexican food except everything is covered in cheese, sauce, and then more cheese. I've never met a human who doesn't enjoy this food. It's perfect for any occasion. Be careful, it's addictive. When you're making this menu, don't forget about the accoutrements. There is something about the vinegar-soaked onions mixed with the ice cold sour cream on top of a hot enchilada that makes you feel all warm and fuzzy inside. Chef Rick Martinez is a man I've had a food crush on for many years in part because he is a Mexican dessert wizard. Prepare for him to cast his tres leches spell on you through his recipe. This meal is incredible, but I would stay within twenty-five feet of a toilet for four to six hours after eating. Trust me.

salsa and accoutrements

PICKLED RED
ONIONS,
page 120

MOVIE
THEATER QUESO,
page 121

GREEN SALSA,
page 121

CHIMICHURRI SAUCE

MAKES 1 CUP

2 cups fresh cilantro leaves

2 cups fresh parsley leaves

2 serrano chilis, stems removed, halved

6 scallions

2 limes

¼ cup red wine vinegar

½ cup olive oil

Kosher salt

Finely chop the herbs, chilis, and scallions. Transfer to a medium bowl and stir in the juice from the limes, red wine vinegar, and olive oil. Season with salt to taste.

PICKLED RED ONIONS

MAKES ½ PINT

1 small red onion, thinly sliced

½ cup red or white wine vinegar

2 teaspoons granulated sugar

½ teaspoon kosher salt

½ teaspoon peppercorns

Pack the onion slices into a half-pint jar or other heatproof container with an airtight lid.

Add the vinegar, sugar, salt, and peppercorns to a small saucepan over high heat. Bring the mixture to a boil and remove from the heat. Pour the hot liquid over the onion and let stand at room temperature until cooled. Cover container and store in the fridge for at least a few hours, up to overnight before serving. Will last, refrigerated, for about 3 weeks.

MOVIE THEATER QUESO

MAKES ABOUT 2 CUPS

I wish it was legal to marry a queso dip. I'd live on a little farm and have small cheesy children and legally change my last name to Queso. Fancy quesos suck—make this one and this one only.

1 (32-ounce) stick Velveeta cheese

1 (10-ounce) can Rotel tomatoes

1 (4-ounce) can pickled jalapeños, chopped

In a small saucepan, combine the Velveeta, tomatoes, and the jalapeños with all their juices. Gently heat over medium, stirring, until melty and warm.

GREEN SALSA

MAKES 2 CUPS

4 medium tomatillos, halved

1 jalapeño

1 serrano chili

½ white onion, chopped

3 cloves garlic

½ avocado

½ cup vegetable oil

1 teaspoon kosher salt

Preheat your broiler. Put tomatillos, chilis, and onion on a sheet pan. Broil until really charred, about 10 to 15 minutes—you want to take it further than you think, but every broiler is different so make sure you keep an eye on it. Add all ingredients to a blender or food processor and process until smooth and emulsified.

MATTY'S CHEESY BEANS

MAKES 6 TO 8

Matty showed me how to make these beans that are really more cheese than beans, but you'll never want to eat beans any other way again. Don't try this with fancy fresh-squeezed juice, just use something sweet like Minute Maid. I have to force myself not to eat the entire thing with a big wooden spoon before serving it.

2 tablespoons vegetable oil

½ white onion, chopped

4 garlic cloves, chopped

2 jalapeños, stems removed, chopped

1 tablespoon ground cumin

1 tablespoon ground coriander

2 tablespoons taco seasoning

1½ cups orange juice

1 (15-ounce) can refried pinto beans

1 (15-ounce) can pinto beans

Salt, to taste

1 pound shredded mozzarella cheese

½ cup sour cream or crema

In a large, deep skillet, heat oil over medium-high. Add the onion, garlic, and jalapeños and cook until the onion is soft and translucent, about 8 minutes. Add the spices and cook until fragrant, about 3 minutes. Add the orange juice and bring to a simmer. Add the beans, salt, cheese, and sour cream and reduce heat to medium. Stir until well combined and warmed through.

MEXICAN RICE

MAKES 6 TO 8

Mexican rice is a little different from other rice because you sort of fry it in oil first. It's perfectly spicy, a little sweet, and a little tangy from the pickled jalapeños.

2 jalapeños

2 tablespoons vegetable oil

½ large white onion, chopped

3 cloves garlic, chopped

2 roma tomatoes, diced

2 tablespoons tomato paste

2 tablespoons ground cumin

2 cups long grain white rice

4 cups water

2 Knorr Tomato Bouillon cubes

2 Knorr Chicken Bouillon cubes

1 cup frozen corn kernels

1 cup pickled jalapeños, chopped

Kosher salt, to taste

Preheat the oven to 450°F.

Using tongs, carefully hold the jalapeños directly over the flame of a burner on the stovetop set to high heat. Allow the flame to char the jalapeños on all sides, about 2 minutes per side. Set aside. Once cool, remove the stems and chop.

Heat a large deep skillet over medium heat. Add the oil, onion, and garlic, and cook until the onion is soft and translucent, about 7 minutes. Add the tomatoes and cook until softened slightly, about 4 minutes. Add the tomato paste, stirring to coat, and cook until slightly thickened, about 2 minutes. Add the cumin and cook until fragrant. Add the rice, and cook until slightly translucent around the edges, about 3 minutes.

Add the water, bouillon cubes, corn, chopped roasted jalapeños, and pickled jalapeños. Raise the heat to high and bring to a boil, mashing the bouillon cubes a bit until fully dissolved. Lower the heat to a simmer and partially cover the pan, cooking until the water is mostly absorbed, about 25 minutes. Remove from the heat, cover completely, and let sit another 15 minutes. Taste, and season with kosher salt if needed.

CHICKEN ENCHILADAS

MAKES 8 TO 10

Enchiladas are basically little burritos smothered in incredible sauce, topped with cheese, then melted. I don't know why I just told you what an enchilada is, because everyone knows what an enchilada is. But I guess if you've never had one, today's the day to try.

1 poblano, halved, seeds and stems removed

6 tomatillos

Peanut, or other neutral oil

1 white onion, chopped

12 garlic cloves, chopped

Pinch of clove

1 tablespoon cumin

Kosher salt and freshly ground pepper, to taste

1 (15-ounce) jar enchilada sauce

1 (4-ounce) can diced green chilis

1 (4-ounce) can pickled nacho jalapeños

1 bunch cilantro

1 cup water

1 (8-ounce) container sour cream

12 corn tortillas

3 cups shredded chicken

1 pound Oaxacan cheese (mozzarella or Monterey Jack can be substituted), shredded

With the rack set in the highest position in your oven, preheat the broiler to high. Add the poblano and tomatillos to a rimmed baking sheet. Broil until charred in places—this can vary as broilers vary greatly in strength. Start checking at 5 minutes, but it could be up to 15.

Turn the oven down to 350°F.

In a small saucepot, add a bit of the peanut oil and heat over medium-high. Add the onion, garlic, clove, cumin, a big pinch of salt, and some freshly ground pepper. Let cook until the onion is soft and translucent, about 7 minutes. Add to a blender and let cool for about 5 to 10 minutes. Add the enchilada sauce, diced green chilis, jalapeños, cilantro, water, and the charred tomatillos and poblanos. Carefully blend on the lowest setting until smooth. Add sour cream and blend again.

Spoon a little sauce onto the bottom of a 9x13-inch baking dish. Roll up each of the tortillas with roughly ¼ cup shredded chicken and about the same amount of cheese, and put seam side down into the dish. Spoon the remaining sauce over the enchiladas and top with the rest of the cheese.

Bake until the cheese is melted and the sauce is bubbling, about 30 minutes. Switch your oven to broil and cook just until there are a few brown spots on the

½ cup queso fresco, crumbled

Lime wedges, crema, sliced radishes, pickled onions, Chimichurri (page 120), and fresh cilantro for serving

gooey cheese. Check often because every broiler is different and this could happen super fast! Serve with your favorite garnishes: lime wedges, more sour cream, radishes, pickled onions, chimichurri, or more cilantro are just a few ideas.

COCONUT TRES LECHES CAKE
with RICK MARTINEZ

MAKES ONE 9-INCH CAKE

Tres leches cake is one of the most rich and decadent desserts you could have. Do not eat this if you are lactose intolerant. Or eat it anyway and suffer the consequences. You've been warned.

FOR THE CAKE

1 orange

1 lime

1 cup evaporated milk

1 cup heavy cream

¾ cup sweetened condensed milk

¼ cup virgin coconut oil, plus more for pan

½ cup unsweetened coconut milk

1¼ cups all-purpose flour

2 teaspoons baking powder

1 teaspoon ground cinnamon

3 large eggs, room temperature

¾ teaspoon kosher salt

¾ cup sugar

1 teaspoon vanilla extract

For the Cake: Using a vegetable peeler, remove zest from orange and lime in wide strips, leaving the white pith behind. Transfer to a large measuring cup or medium bowl. Whisk in the evaporated milk, cream, and sweetened condensed milk. Let sit until ready to use.

Arrange a rack in the center of the oven. Preheat the oven to 350°F. Grease the bottom of a springform pan with oil. Heat the coconut milk and remaining ¼ cup oil in a small saucepan over medium, stirring, until oil is melted. Let cool on a wire rack for at least 30 minutes.

Whisk the flour, baking powder, and cinnamon in a small bowl. Sift through a fine-mesh sieve onto a piece of parchment or wax paper.

Using an electric mixer on low speed, beat the eggs in a large bowl, gradually increasing speed to medium-high, until broken up. Add the salt and continue to beat until beginning to foam. Reduce the mixer speed to low and gradually add the sugar, then increase the speed to high and beat until very light and pale yellow, about 3 to 4 minutes. Reduce the mixer speed to low and beat in the cooled milk mixture and vanilla until combined. Gradually add the dry ingredients, using the parchment to help you pour in a steady stream without getting it all over the outside of the machine, and continue to beat on low until no lumps remain, about another minute. Scrape the sides and bottom

¾ cup sugar

¼ cup water

3 egg whites, room
temperature

¼ teaspoon cream of
tartar

¼ teaspoon kosher salt

⅓ cup toasted coconut
flakes, for garnish

of the bowl with a spatula, give batter a good stir, then scrape into prepared pan.

Bake the cake until the top is golden and a toothpick inserted into the center comes out clean, about 15 to 25 minutes. Let cool for 30 minutes.

Using a wooden skewer, poke holes into the entire surface of the cake, making sure the skewer hits the bottom of the pan. Hold the zest back with a wooden spoon while you slowly pour some of the milk-zest mixture over the cake, allowing the milk to be absorbed by the cake before pouring more. Discard zest. Cover with foil or plastic wrap and chill for 8 to 12 hours.

For the Frosting and Cake Assembly: Fit a small saucepan with a candy thermometer. Bring sugar and water to a boil. Continue to cook, occasionally swirling syrup in pan, until thermometer registers 240°F.

Meanwhile, using an electric mixer on high speed, beat the egg whites in a medium bowl until medium peaks form. As soon as the syrup reaches 240°F, with mixer on medium-low speed, pour the syrup in a slow, steady stream over egg whites and beat until incorporated. Add the cream of tartar and salt. Increase the speed to high and beat meringue until thick and glossy stiff peaks form, about 4 minutes (bowl will be warm to the touch).

Run an offset spatula around the edges of the springform pan to loosen cake. Using a fish spatula or two large spatulas, carefully transfer cake to a platter.

Using an offset spatula or the back of a spoon, spread the meringue over the top and sides of the cake, swirling decoratively. Toast meringue with a kitchen torch, if desired. Sprinkle with toasted coconut flakes.

f*ck morton's
steakhouse

I don't usually go to steakhouses because they pretty much all suck. Most steakhouses either have a great vibe and shitty food or shitty food and a great vibe. Plus they charge you like a hundred dollars for a steak you could buy at any supermarket for a fraction of the price. Fuck a place like Morton's Steakhouse—just go to a local butcher, get some nice meat, sprinkle it with salt and pepper, sear the fuck out of it, then come find me and give me a kiss.

For the last ten or so years I have rented a house with a bunch of friends for New Year's to vanish from the public eye for a week. Last year we made this exact meal and took a bunch of mushrooms. My friend Ben said we should put on a fake *SNL* and he would be the host. It took a while to get everyone to go along with the plan, but once we finally did, he froze and completely blew it. My brother's wife Evi did too many mushrooms and kept looking at her hands and threatening to jump into the fireplace. I think I may have eaten the entire cheese plate alone but somehow didn't poop my pants. It was a Christmas miracle and it wasn't even Christmas.

I remember this one time I went to a fancy steakhouse called the Grill in New York City. It's a legendary mid-century room in the Seagram Building. It's the kind of place that you feel like you don't want to touch anything because it's all so beautiful, but actually the room is so big and sturdy that you can get rowdy and no one will notice. Time seems to melt when you're there and you walk out four hours later full of six martinis, an entire bottle of wine, and so much cream and meat coursing through your small intestines that trying to squeeze out a fart becomes a game of Russian roulette.

After the meal, we stuffed all nine of us into a little clown car and listened to Smash Mouth's "All Star" six times in a row and then stumbled out into the streets of Chinatown before walking into my friend Emile's apartment (which is a six-story walk-up . . . there should be a game where if you eat at the Grill and make it to the top without shitting your pants, confetti shoots out of the ceiling and you get a gift card to a fancy spa). It turned into a party and Ed Sheeran kept playing UK garage and making air horn noises with his mouth. My friend Nico came by with Tiger Hood (an amazing man who is known for creating a game where you hit milk cartons into a box with a golf club, it's so fun). Ed had just opened a bottle of wine that cost more than a car, but I convinced him to come down and play with us. I'll never forget drinking it out of the bottle while smelling rotting trash as Eric André did whip-its while Nico sunk a shot from fifty feet away as a hundred innocent bystanders cheered as if we had just won the US Open. Only in New York City, baby!

Make this menu for a date or a group of people and I promise you, you'll make some memories.

BEST POTATOES EVER

SERVES 8 TO 10

I'm pretty sure that when I die I won't be remembered for my music but for these perfect potatoes. I'm not just saying this because it's my cookbook, it's because I'm positive this is the best potato you will ever put in your mouth.

3 pounds russet potatoes, peeled and cut into 1- to 2-inch wedges

Neutral oil or beef tallow, for frying

Kosher salt

½ cup mayonnaise

½ tablespoon smoked paprika

½ tablespoon lemon juice

Black pepper, to taste

Fill a large pot with about 1 inch of water and place a steamer basket into the pot. Bring the water to a boil. Add the potatoes and steam until they are really really mushy, about 45 minutes.

When potatoes are cooked, carefully drain and let rest in the pot for about 30 seconds to allow excess moisture to evaporate. Transfer the potatoes to a big stainless-steel bowl and shake like crazy, until a thick layer of mashed potato–like paste has built up on the potato chunks. Transfer potatoes to a large, rimmed baking sheet and separate them, spreading them out evenly, and put in the freezer until frozen, about an hour or overnight. Once completely frozen, you can transfer to a ziplock bag and use whenever.

Set deep fryer to 375°F, or prepare a large deep pot with oil for frying and bring up to 375°F.

Working in batches, fry the potatoes until super crispy and deep golden brown, about 8 minutes. Transfer to paper towel–lined plates and sprinkle with plenty of salt.

In a small bowl, combine the mayonnaise, paprika, and lemon juice. Stir well to combine. Season with a bit of salt and pepper to taste.

LITTLE SALMON ROE TOASTS

MAKES 8

There's this tiny restaurant in New York called ZZ's Clam Bar and I always end up there late night. Once I was there and they were passing out these little roe toasts. I was so drunk and they were so good that I just took them all and put them in my pocket because I didn't know when I would be back in New York again. I was an actual maniac. I didn't even wrap them, it was just loose crème fraîche and roe bits schmeared in my pocket, but they came in handy at 3 a.m., smooshed or not.

8 slices King's Hawaiian bread, toasted

¼ cup crème fraîche

2 tablespoons honey

4 ounces salmon roe

¼ cup chives, cut into 1-inch pieces

Pink peppercorns and lemon zest, for sprinkling

Cut the crust off your toast and then cut into two little rectangles. Next, spoon on a little crème fraîche and then the honey. Top with a bunch of salmon roe, some pretty little chives, peppercorns, and lemon zest and get ready to have your mind blown.

CAESAR SALAD

SERVES 6 TO 8

The real caesar salad was invented in Tijuana by an Italian chef. I've had that one—they use lime instead of lemon. My brother Jer is always in search of the best caesar. I made this one for him and he said it was the greatest he's ever had, and I've never been able to beat my brother in anything. I guess this counts as beating him in a caesar-off.

FOR THE CROUTONS

¼ cup olive oil

4 tablespoons butter

½ loaf sourdough, cut into 2-inch pieces

½ cup white wine

1 lemon, zested, reserve half for juice

¼ cup parmesan cheese, grated

Kosher salt and freshly ground black pepper

¼ cup parsley, finely chopped

FOR THE DRESSING

1 head garlic

Extra virgin olive oil

½ cup mayonnaise

1 tablespoon grainy mustard

6 to 8 anchovies

1 lemon, zested and juiced

Kosher salt and freshly ground black pepper

For the Croutons: In a large skillet, heat the oil and 2 tablespoons of butter over medium. Lay the bread chunks in a single layer. Flip and add white wine and the remaining 2 tablespoons butter.

Squeeze in the juice of half a lemon and sprinkle with parmesan cheese. Season with salt and pepper to taste. Stir to combine. Let the bread chunks sit and continue cooking until charred on one side and the liquid is mostly evaporated.

Remove from the pan and sprinkle with the lemon zest and parsley, and let dry out for at least 20 minutes before serving.

For the Dressing: Preheat the oven to 425°F. Cut the top third off the head of garlic. Place it on a small parchment-lined piece of foil and drizzle with olive oil. Roast until fragrant and the cloves are super soft and golden brown, about 45 minutes. Let cool until you can safely handle it. Squeeze the garlic cloves into the bowl of a food processor. Add the mayo, mustard, anchovies, lemon zest and juice, and blend until smooth. Taste for seasoning and adjust with a bit of salt and pepper. Set dressing aside.

FOR THE SALAD

Caesar Dressing

2 heads radicchio

2 heads little gem lettuce

Croutons

Parmesan cheese, for serving

Lemons, cut into wedges for serving

Boquerones (white anchovies)

To Assemble the Salad: Put a bit of the dressing into a large bowl. Add the washed and torn greens and mix to combine. Add more dressing if desired. Pile the salad high with croutons, grated parmesan, lemon wedges, and boquerones.

BEST
POTATOES
EVER,
page 135

CREAMED SPINACH

SERVES 6 TO 8

Whenever I make creamed spinach, I feel like I've got way too much spinach, but when you cook down 4 pounds it's the size of a silver dollar you can fit in your pocket. Anyway, this thing I'm sure has more cream than spinach, and that's why it's so good.

4 pounds spinach

4 tablespoons unsalted butter

¼ cup all-purpose flour

2 cups half and half

1 (8-ounce) block cream cheese, cut into 1-inch cubes

1 cup parmesan cheese, grated

Kosher salt and freshly ground black pepper

Pinch nutmeg

Bring a big pot of water to a boil, and salt it heavily so it tastes like the sea. Meanwhile, prepare an ice bath in a big bowl with a bunch of ice and some water. Add the spinach to the pot, and let it cook just for a second until it wilts. Remove it with tongs or a spider and plunge it into the ice bath.

In a large skillet, melt the butter over medium-high heat. Whisk in the flour and just cook the flour, about 1 minute. Slowly, while whisking, add in the half and half. Once it's smooth and combined, start adding in the cream cheese and then the parmesan, and mix until completely melted and smooth. Season to taste with salt and pepper.

Remove the spinach from the ice bath and dry it out on a clean kitchen towel or just sort of squeeze the water out with your hands, and then stir it into the creamy mixture. Taste for seasoning again and add a pinch of nutmeg.

JAH MAMA SHRIMP

SERVES 8

My friends Jah and Josh Blum made these incredible shrimp at our friend's house. Jah has a hot sauce that's so good (I have it listed in the My Kitchen section). Get it because you need it in this recipe and on top of every single thing in the world. If you can find fresh langoustines it makes this dish truly spectacular. Cooking them in the shell protects the inside so they stay juicy and moist.

FOR THE SALSA VERDE

1 bunch fresh mint
(1 cup packed)

½ bunch fresh basil (2 cups)

1 bunch chives

¼ cup tarragon

2 jalapeños or serrano
chilis, stems and seeds
removed

6 cloves garlic

1 red onion

½ cup Champagne or
white wine vinegar

2 tablespoons freshly
squeezed lemon juice

2 cups olive oil

1 tablespoon Jah Mama
hot sauce

Kosher salt

FOR THE SHRIMP

2 pounds prawns, tails
split in half

Extra virgin olive oil

Kosher salt and black
pepper

1 recipe Salsa Verde

Lemons, for serving

For the Salsa Verde: Chop up the herbs, chilis, garlic, and onion by hand, very finely. Add to a medium bowl. Stir in the vinegar, lemon juice, olive oil, and Jah Mama sauce. Season to taste with salt.

For the Shrimp: Preheat the grill to 450°F.

Drizzle the shrimp with oil and season with salt and pepper.

Grill the shrimp until cooked through, about 6 minutes, until the shells are bright pink and the meat is opaque throughout. This will vary depending on the size of your prawns.

Serve with Salsa Verde and a big squeeze of lemon.

PERFECT STEAK THREE WAYS

There are many ways to make the perfect steak. Here are three. Some of these methods are more complex than others but I guarantee you there's one here for you. This steak is kind of like reverse searing, but you're smoking it for a while so you get all of those carcinogens that we really shouldn't be having. All that smoke flavor seeps into the meat and you take it out and put it in a pan to get the perfect sear on the outside. I'm not a grill marks type of guy. I don't care. When I was a kid, my family was always like, "We gotta see the grill marks!" Fuck the grill marks, they're overrated. Order your steak from Pat LaFrieda on Goldbelly. My favorite cuts to do this with are filet and rib-eye—I like doing a mix because one is fatty and one is super tender and a little bit leaner. My steaks are usually about 1½ inches thick and about 20 ounces each for rib-eyes and skirt steaks, 8 ounces each for filet.

Smoked: Set your Traeger (or smoker of choice) to 225°F Super Smoke.

Season the steak generously with salt and pepper. Once it reaches an internal temperature of 120°F to 125°F (about an hour), remove. Preheat a flat-top grill or cast-iron skillet over high heat. Sear the steak on the flat-top or in the cast-iron until medium-rare, about 125°F on an instant read thermometer or about 2 to 4 minutes per side depending on the thickness of your meat. Melt in 4 tablespoons of butter and baste until it reaches desired doneness. To finish, cover a big cutting board with a generous amount of olive oil, your favorite crunchy salt, and a little lemon juice, and chop up any herbs you might have on hand. Slice into half-inch chunks against the grain, then place over the mixture and then kind of toss it all together to serve.

Sous vide: Season the steak with salt and pepper, fresh rosemary, and garlic if you have it. Seal in a ziplock bag. Look up instructions on your sous vide machine—I usually set mine to 115°F. Finish same as above.

Seared: I like to sear skirt steaks.

Season generously with salt and pepper. Let the steak marinate for at least one hour and up to overnight in a mixture containing the juice of 1 orange, juice of 1 lime, 1 cup Coca-Cola, 1 cup Modelo, a handful of chopped cilantro stems, ½ teaspoon ground cumin, and ½ teaspoon Chef Merito Steak & Meat Seasoning.

Heat 1 tablespoon neutral oil in a cast-iron skillet over high heat. Add the steak and cook until medium-rare (130°F on an instant read thermometer), about 4 minutes per side. Serve with melted butter and more flaky salt.

STRAWBERRIES AND CREAM

SERVES 8 TO 10

Making homemade whipped cream is time-consuming and takes some elbow grease, but it is far superior than the shit you get in the store.

1 cup heavy cream

1 tablespoon confectioners' sugar

2 pounds of the best strawberries you can find

In a large bowl or the bowl of an electric stand mixer fitted with the whisk attachment, beat the cream and sugar until soft peaks form, about 3 minutes. This means when you take the whisk out of the cream and flip it upside-down, the little peak on the end should be floppy. Keep a close eye on it, you don't want it to get too stiff. Serve with strawberries.

kibitz and complain

While I was growing up, there were only three times I was allowed to have a soda. 1) Flat Coca-Cola if I was puking. 2) Ginger ale if I was on an airplane. 3) Dr. Brown's Cream Soda if I was at a Jewish deli with my dad. He always got Black Cherry or Cel-Ray. I don't even really like soda—it's too spicy for me. But I get one anytime I'm eating the chosen people's food.

If you're Jewish, which I am, you will fight with your friends about whether Katz's or 2nd Ave Deli is better. You could be eating the best meal of your life, but still the only conversation at the dinner table would be what you're going to have for lunch the next day. I'm convinced that someone crushes up Xanax and sneaks it into every Reuben across the globe.

Don't eat this meal if you're on a diet or have a date later, unless your date also ate a mouthful of whitefish, in which case make out with them and make my "I Hope We Didn't Make a Baby" Breakfast Burrito when you wake up.

WHITEFISH DIP *with* BAGEL CHIPS

MAKES ABOUT 2½ CUPS

1 whole smoked whitefish, skin and pinbones removed, flaked (about 3 cups)

⅓ cup mayo

3 tablespoons sour cream

1 lemon, zested, plus the juice of half a lemon

1 bunch dill, finely chopped

3 dashes Tabasco, or more to taste

Kosher salt

Freshly cracked pepper

Bagel chips, for serving

Don't be scared of a smoked fish dip. Just shut up and eat it.

In a large bowl combine the flaked whitefish, mayo, sour cream, lemon zest, lemon juice, dill, and Tabasco. Mix it well, and sort of mash it all up. Taste it before you season because you might not need more salt. But add pepper. Serve with bagel chips.

MATZO BALL SOUP

SERVES 4 TO 6

Every Jewish person claims their grandmother makes the best matzo ball soup, but my favorite grandma died and took her recipe to the grave, and my other grandmother was a monster (when I told her I loved her she told me love was a strong word) and didn't know how to cook. So I got my brother's Polish wife Evi to give me her recipe. It's so good (my mom thinks it's too salty).

FOR THE BROTH

1 heirloom or free-range chicken, cut into 8 pieces

4 carrots, peeled and roughly chopped

3 celery stalks, roughly chopped

Kosher salt

1 tablespoon black peppercorns

2 dried bay leaves, or 4 fresh

Handful of parsley stems

1 tablespoon kosher salt

Place all the broth ingredients in a large pot and cover with 3 inches of cold water. Bring to a boil, reduce heat, and simmer, skimming the surface occasionally, 3½ to 4 hours.

Remove chicken pieces to a plate to cool, then strain the broth and return to a clean pot (you should have 6 to 8 cups). Discard the solids. When the chicken is cool enough to handle, shred the meat and set aside.

Make matzo balls according to package instructions. I like to add Vegeta seasoning and chopped parsley to the matzo ball mix for extra flavor.

Bring broth back to a simmer and add the carrots and celery. Season with salt and pepper. Cook until vegetables are tender, 10 to 15 minutes. Add shredded chicken back to the pot and stir in more Vegeta to taste. Vegeta is a European all-purpose seasoning that is typically used in soups and is my secret for extra flavor. If you are sensitive to MSG, they have one without it as well. It is salty, so make sure you add a little at a time. I like to add 1½ teaspoons to start, then add more as needed.

1 box Manischewitz Matzo Ball Mix

2 tablespoons vegetable oil

2 large eggs

2 teaspoons Vegeta, or more to taste

1 teaspoon parsley, chopped

4 to 5 carrots, peeled and thinly sliced (2 cups)

3 celery stalks, thinly sliced (1½ cups)

Salt and pepper to taste

Meat from chicken (about 4 packed cups)

Chopped dill and parsley, for serving

Place a matzo ball or two in a bowl and ladle soup over the top. Garnish with lots of chopped parsley and dill.

If making ahead, store soup and matzo balls separately. You can hold matzo balls on a small parchment-lined pan covered with plastic wrap in the refrigerator.

MOM'S KUGEL

SERVES 8 TO 10

My mom can't cook, but I think when you turn fifty, the Jewish fairy puts a perfect kugel recipe and all the ingredients in your pantry. My brother doesn't like raisins so my mom never put them in her kugel. You can if you want to . . . but I think he might be right.

1 (12-ounce) package extra-wide egg noodles

½ cup milk

½ cup granulated sugar

2 cups (16 ounces) cottage cheese

2 cups sour cream

2 large eggs

1 tablespoon vanilla

Kosher salt

½ cup unsalted butter

½ cup dark brown sugar

2 cups Kellogg's Cornflakes, smashed to crumbs

Preheat the oven to 450°F.

Cook the noodles in a large pot of salted water according to the package directions, strain, and return to the pot. Whisk together the milk, sugar, cottage cheese, sour cream, eggs, vanilla, and a generous pinch of salt. Stir in the butter and mix until it is melted and fully coating the noodles. Stir in the milk mixture and toss to coat.

In a small bowl, stir together the brown sugar and cornflake crumbs.

Butter a 9x13-inch glass baking dish and transfer noodle mixture to dish. Sprinkle with cornflake mixture. Bake until golden brown, about 20 minutes.

CABBAGE ROLLS

SERVES 6 TO 8

More than anything in my book, a cabbage roll might be the best thing to make ahead of time and freeze. I make fifty at a time, reheat them later, and give them a new home in my stomach.

1 large or 2 medium heads green cabbage, about 3 pounds

2 onions, chopped

6 cloves garlic, chopped

2 tablespoons unsalted butter

Kosher salt and freshly ground black pepper

2 pounds ground beef (80 percent fat)

¾ cup uncooked white rice

2 eggs

1 (14-ounce) can crushed tomatoes

1 cup water

½ cup chopped golden raisins

1 cup granulated sugar, plus 1 tablespoon for baking

½ cup ketchup

3 lemons, juiced

1 orange, juiced

½ cup sauerkraut

½ cup white wine vinegar

½ tablespoon cinnamon

Remove the core from the cabbage and separate into leaves. Blanch a few at a time in salted boiling water until pliable, 1 to 2 minutes per batch. When cool enough to handle, use a knife to remove the ribs. Chop 1 cup cabbage and reserve for later.

Cook onions and garlic in 2 tablespoons butter and a large pinch of salt over medium heat, stirring occasionally, until softened, about 10 minutes.

Combine beef, rice, eggs, and half the sauteed onion mixture. Season with 1 tablespoon of salt and some fresh pepper.

Add a little handful of the mixture to each cabbage leaf and carefully roll it like a little burrito, folding up the sides to create a little package.

To make the sauce, combine the remaining onion mixture, crushed tomatoes, water, raisins, sugar, ketchup, lemon juice, orange juice, chopped cabbage, sauerkraut, vinegar, and cinnamon. Season with salt and pepper.

Put a thin layer of the sauce at the bottom of a 9x13-inch pan. Tightly pack the cabbage rolls in the pan, and then add the remaining sauce. You want them to be swimming.

Sprinkle with 1 tablespoon sugar.

Place a rimmed baking sheet lined with foil on lower rack to catch any drips. Bake cabbage on center rack at 350°F until meat is falling apart and rice is cooked, 2 to 2½ hours. Tent with foil if getting too dark.

REUBEN *with* ADAM PERRY LANG'S HOMEMADE PASTRAMI

For those of you who don't know what a Reuben is, it's a sandwich with some sort of smoked meat (usually pastrami) topped with sauerkraut and melted Swiss cheese then smothered with Russian dressing. It is the sandwich equivalent of taking a horse tranquilizer. My friend Adam Perry Lang, a legendary meat whisperer, has been gracious enough to clog our arteries with this incredible pastrami recipe.

FOR THE BRINE

2½ gallons distilled water

10 cloves garlic, smashed

¼ cup black peppercorns, smashed

1 tablespoon crushed red pepper

5 fresh bay leaves, crushed

1 tablespoon allspice, smashed

30 grams/2 tablespoons Prague powder #1, also known as pink curing salt (this is a salt made for curing meat)

2½ cups kosher salt

1½ cup white sugar

7- to 10-pound brisket (prime packers cut brisket with the fat cap on; ask your butcher for a thicker flat)

To make the brine: Add a half gallon of the water to a very large pot and add the garlic, peppercorns, crushed red pepper, bay leaves, and allspice. Bring to a boil over high heat for a minute or two to activate the flavor.

Remove the water mixture from the heat, then add the Prague powder, salt, and white sugar, stirring for a minute or two to dissolve. Add the remaining water to further dissolve the mixture. Transfer to a Cambro (or other large nonreactive container like a large plastic bin with a lid that will fit inside your fridge) and allow to cool to room temperature. After cooling to room temp, the brine is ready to use. This is your finished brine.

Submerge the brisket into the finished brine so that the brisket is fully covered in the brine. It's best to do this in a large bag so you have 360-degree coverage but you can alternatively place the brisket in a pot or dish, as long as it is completely covered. You can place a heavy plate over the brisket to keep it submerged. Put the brisket into the fridge and allow to brine for 5 to 7 days.

(continued)

**FOR THE PASTRAMI
DRY RUB**

1 cup black peppercorns

½ cup coriander seeds

½ cup light brown sugar,
packed

¼ cup paprika

2 tablespoons garlic
powder

2 tablespoons onion
powder

To make the dry rub: Lightly toast peppercorns in a pan
until aromatic, then place in spice mill and grind until
somewhat coarse but not too coarse . . . it needs to be
uniform. Repeat with coriander seeds. Add to a bowl with
remaining dry rub ingredients and stir until well combined.

To make the pastrami: When ready to smoke, remove the
brisket from the brine and give it a quick rinse. Lightly pat
it dry, then cover all over on both sides with dry rub.

Preheat the Traeger (or your smoker of choice) to 225°F.
Put a baking dish filled with water in the bottom rack of
the smoker.

FOR THE PASTRAMI

¼ cup duck fat (ask your butcher for this—often it is rendered and shelf stable so you'll find it in the oil section of your grocery store)

1 cup Mott's Original Apple Juice

FOR THE RUSSIAN DRESSING

Makes about 1 pint

1 cup mayo

¼ cup red onion, finely chopped

1¼ tablespoons horseradish

¾ cup ketchup

1 teaspoon Worcestershire sauce

3 big pinches smoked paprika

1 teaspoon Frank's RedHot

½ tablespoon sugar

Place the brisket in the smoker with the fat cap (this is the thick white layer of fat on the brisket) pointing up. Cook until it has a beautiful crust and an internal temperature of 160°F, which will take about 3 to 4 hours.

Carefully place the brisket on a large piece of foil and slowly add duck fat and apple juice. Then wrap tightly to seal it all up!

Place back in the Traeger or the oven set to 300°F until an internal temperature of 203°F is reached, about 3 to 4 hours more.

Remove and place on a cooling rack until cool enough to handle but still warm, about 45 minutes, then unwrap, remove the brisket, and transfer to a sheet pan. Defat the cooking liquid by skimming the fat off the top of the liquid with a fat strainer, spoon, or turkey baster.

Wrap in plastic wrap or vacuum seal with some of the defatted liquid, wrap that in a beach towel, and place in a cooler with no ice (or the fridge on a baking sheet) and allow to rest for 1 hour.

Remove and thinly slice against the grain.

To make the Russian Dressing: Add all the ingredients to a bowl and whisk to combine.

(continued)

FOR THE REUBENS

Unsalted butter

Mayonnaise

Seeded rye bread

Russian Dressing

Pastrami

2 cups sauerkraut

½ pound Swiss cheese, sliced

To make the Reubens: Preheat your broiler.

In a small saucepan, melt a little butter over medium heat.

Rub a little mayo on the outside of both slices of bread. Place the bread in the pan, mayo side down, and let get crispy, about 2 minutes. Spread a thick layer of Russian Dressing on the inside of both pieces of bread.

Pile on an actual tower of pastrami. Make a mountain of sauerkraut and cover with two slices of Swiss cheese.

Pop under the broiler until cheese is melted, about 2 minutes.

Add more dressing if you need to. Then unhinge your jaw and get ready to enter the ultimate food coma. Like really, clear your day after this one, you're not going to be able to move. Every muscle in your body will turn into melt-in-your-mouth tender pastrami.

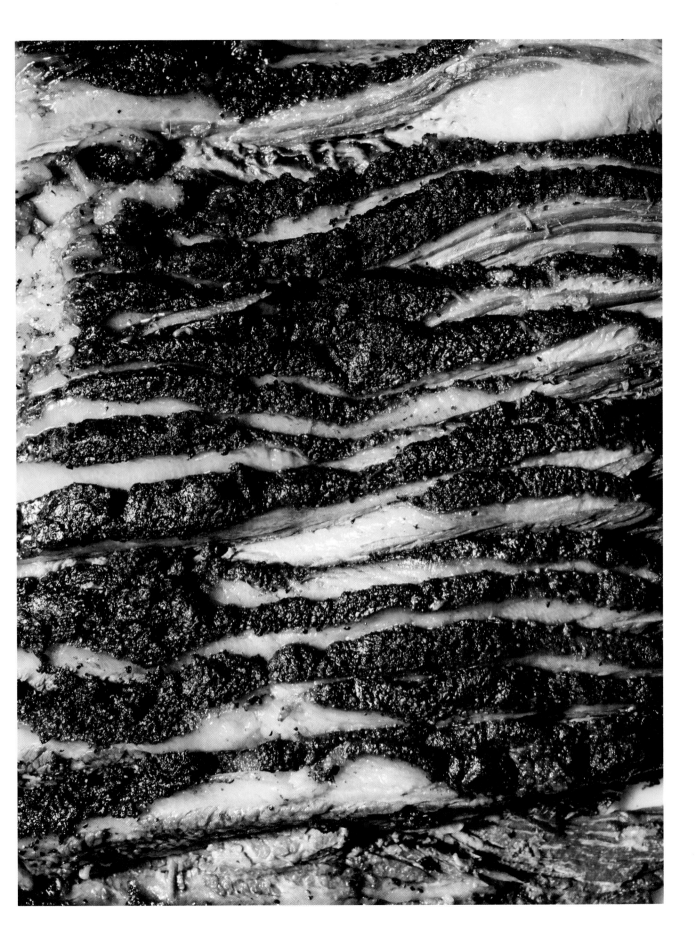

RUGELACH

MAKES 4 DOZEN

So many people have their own variations of rugelach. I really like the simple cream cheese dough, don't give me any of that fancy shit. Just give me the easy one that my grandmother Mimi made.

FOR THE DOUGH

8 ounces cream cheese, room temperature

2 sticks unsalted butter, room temperature

¼ cup granulated sugar

¼ teaspoon kosher salt

1 teaspoon vanilla extract

2 cups all-purpose flour

FOR THE FILLING

½ cup heavy cream

4 ounces dark chocolate, chopped

2 tablespoons cocoa powder

2 tablespoons unsalted butter

½ cup Nutella

1 cup walnuts, finely chopped

¼ cup dark brown sugar

2 teaspoons cinnamon

1 egg

1 tablespoon heavy cream

For the Dough: In the bowl of a stand mixer fitted with the paddle attachment, beat the cream cheese and butter together until light and fluffy, about 4 minutes. Add the sugar, pinch of salt, and vanilla, and continue to beat, about 2 minutes. Slowly add the flour and mix, another 2 minutes. Form the dough into a ball and cut into 4 pieces. Wrap tightly with plastic and refrigerate for an hour.

For the Filling: In a small pot, heat the cream over medium-high until simmering. Remove from the heat. Place the chocolate in a bowl and pour the cream over it. Stir until melted. Stir in the cocoa powder, then the butter. Stir in the Nutella and set aside to cool.

In a separate small bowl, combine the walnuts, dark brown sugar, cinnamon, and a pinch of salt.

To assemble the rugelach: Roll each of the dough balls into a 9-inch circle. Spread with the chocolate filling (4 tablespoons), and then sprinkle with a quarter of the walnut mixture, leaving a ¼-inch border. Cut each circle into 12 wedges. Roll each wedge, starting from the wide end, moving in toward the center. Tuck the little point under the roll and arrange on a parchment-lined baking sheet. Chill for 30 minutes.

Preheat the oven to 350°F. Combine egg and cream and beat to combine. Brush the rugelach with the egg wash and sprinkle with sugar. Bake until golden brown, about 15 to 20 minutes. Let cool on a wire rack.

Store rugelach in an airtight container for up to three days.

perfect picnic

A picnic is something you rarely do, but once you're doing it, you love it. Take time and effort to create the perfect experience for your mom, friend, or someone you're trying to *schtup*, this is supposed to be special.

Don't bring anything that's going to get soggy and limp like an old man's weiner. Get a cute bag to carry everything, something functional but also cool to look at. The cuter the better. Maybe it's a little basket, a nice dish towel, or a handkerchief from your house. But don't actually go out and buy something because there are so many things around the house that can serve as your bag.

Wrap everything separately and wrap your silverware, it goes a long way. Bring some special napkins, a water bottle (to fill with water or some liquid courage), and always bring a Bluetooth speaker. Nothing is worse than sitting in silence while eating a cheese plate.

One time I was with my friend Becky for her birthday. A friend had shown me an amazing hike in the mountains of Malibu the week before and I wanted to show her how cool it was. My plan was to hike to the top and eat some yummy snacks. It was a secret path so there was no road or map. We wound up getting lost for hours and never found the top, so we decided to just have our picnic right then and there. When I reached into my bag I realized I had forgotten all the food. The moral of the story is, I fucked up, ruined my friend's birthday, and we almost died of dehydration. The good news is I learned from those mistakes and put a plan in place for you to look like an absolute hero. You're welcome.

HOW TO MAKE A CHEESE PLATE

Fruit

You need a fruit for your cheese plate and it needs to be perfect. Don't go and buy some shitty peach that's the size of my head and has stickers all over it. Go to the farmers market, or somewhere you can get something organic. You can cut many corners, but with fruit and cheese you need to shell out some shekels. Find out what's in season, and change it up—grapes, pears, persimmons, pomegranates, even slices of orange can be great.

Cheese

Find a local cheese shop nearby and if you can't, go somewhere they at least care a little bit more and you're not getting Kraft to sprinkle on top of a cracker. Try to get a few different types of cheeses. My favorites are cheeses that have little delicious crystals that melt in your mouth, like an aged Beemster gouda or Mimolette. You'll also want something sharp like a cheddar— my favorite is something really aged like Cabot Clothbound or Hook's. Also grab something soft like goat cheese or a brie. Then you want something a little sweet like jam, honey, or some quince paste to tie it all together. Maybe you want some almonds or something else that's crunchy, even corn nuts.

Crackers

I like to get a few different types of crackers and slice a fresh baguette or crusty sourdough. I love fruit and nut crackers, like Jans or Raincoast Crisps.

For presentation, make sure you have a nice big board or platter. Cluster colorful fruits and any nuts together on the board so they are easy to grab, and make sure that there is enough room for people to access the cheese without touching everything else. Make sure to have cute little knives if you need them, or pre-slice the cheese. Add fresh herbs or citrus leaves, or even edible flowers for a little extra something something. And find a really good spot in the shade.

GAZPACHO

MAKES 2 QUARTS

My friend Simon might be one of the most interesting men on planet Earth. It's kind of hard to pinpoint exactly what he does, but I think he may just do everything exceptionally well. He owns a record store and bookstore, he used to have an underground supper club, he's created the menus for tons of restaurants, he worked for the most pretentious galleries in NYC and is a fabulous fine artist himself, and he's a professional hater of all things . . . you get what I mean. A man of many talents. A couple of years ago I was with my mom in New York about to see some art but she was hungry and made sure I knew it every three to six minutes. Simon gave her a small bowl of this gazpacho, and my mother proceeded to drink about a gallon's worth of it until she was as full as a bull. The end.

3 pounds ripe tomatoes (overripe and blemished tomatoes are good for this recipe, as is using a mix of different tomatoes like Sungold, Super Sweet 100, heirloom, etc.)

1½ pounds cucumbers (Korean or Persian cucumbers are best here)

1 pound bell peppers (red, orange, and yellow are best, but green will work)

3 cloves garlic

½ medium sweet onion

Salt and pepper, to taste

3 slices crusty white bread

1 to 1½ cups extra virgin olive oil

Roughly chop the vegetables and place them in a large bowl with 2 tablespoons salt and 1 tablespoon freshly cracked black pepper. Cover and macerate at least 2 hours, up to 8, tossing occasionally.

Tear the bread (I like sourdough but any crusty white bread will work) into large pieces and toss with the macerated vegetables. Push and squeeze the bread to the bottom of the bowl to soak up the accumulated vegetable juices. Let sit another 30 minutes.

Blend (in batches if necessary) while streaming in the best quality extra virgin olive oil you can find. The idea is to make a thick emulsion with the bread, vegetables, and olive oil. You may need to add a small amount of water to help with the blending. Don't add too much, but some splashes are absolutely fine. The soup will lighten in color as you add the oil, almost like a vinaigrette. Once blended, strain through a fine meshed sieve, discarding any solids that remain like pepper or tomato skins and under-processed bread.

2 tablespoons sherry vinegar, or more to taste

Fried breadcrumbs, fresh basil leaves, cherry tomatoes, and chopped cucumber for serving

Whisk in good quality sherry vinegar to the puree to start, and taste for seasoning and balance. You'll probably need more salt and pepper. I honestly don't know how much vinegar I usually add, I do it totally by taste. It might be up to ¼ cup. I don't think it's more than that. It should be tangy but still very vegetal and fresh. Like a delicious liquid salad! You tasted it so you know. Chill in the refrigerator at least 4 hours, garnish, and serve. This soup is *definitely* better chilled overnight and eaten the next day. It also lasts in the fridge about a week—just shake it up well before you serve it again.

"I MIGHT GO VEGETARIAN" VEGGIE SANDWICH

SERVES 8 (HALF A SANDWICH EACH)

I know what you're thinking: why would I have this sandwich when I can just have a huge chicken parmesan? First of all, the bread on a chicken parmesan is going to look like water by the time you get to it. There's nothing worse than a soggy sandwich. This sandwich is crisp, refreshing, and delicious, and the cheddar cheese on top gives you that fat that you just need. It's the type of sandwich that makes you not even miss meat. I would eat this on a picnic blanket or sitting on my couch watching reruns of Curb Your Enthusiasm.

¼ cup mayo

2 heaping tablespoons whole grain mustard

8 slices sourdough bread

1 avocado, sliced

Squeeze of lemon juice

2 Persian cucumbers, thinly sliced

½ cup alfalfa sprouts

Drizzle olive oil

Kosher salt and freshly ground pepper

½ cup pickled cherry peppers, sliced

1 kosher dill pickle, thinly sliced

4 thin slices really good sharp cheddar cheese (like Cabot Clothbound)

In a small bowl, combine the mayo and mustard. Spread a little on every slice of bread. Arrange some of the avocado on four slices of bread, squeeze a little lemon on top; then arrange the cucumbers, then the sprouts. Drizzle with a little olive oil and salt and pepper. Keep building the sandwiches with the peppers, pickles, and cheese, and then top with the remaining bread.

CURRIED CHICKEN SALAD SANDWICH

MAKES 1 QUART

Curried Chicken Salad is something that you kind of forget about, and then you have it and it blows your mind. The sweet and savory combo gets me every time.

1 pound (3 cups) shredded chicken from 1 rotisserie chicken

2½ tablespoons curry powder

½ cup golden raisins (chopped if large)

½ cup scallions, green part only, thinly sliced

1 cup mayonnaise

¼ cup apricot preserves

2 tablespoons finely chopped cornichon

Kosher salt and freshly ground black pepper

Baguette, for serving

Handful arugula, for serving

Shred chicken using your hands or two forks. Combine all ingredients except for the bread in a large bowl and mash it together with a fork. The mushier the better. Place a dollop on a piece of bread and top with some arugula and another piece of bread.

SALTED CARAMEL RICE KRISPIES TREATS™

MAKES 16

Rice Krispies Treats™ are a sleeper dessert item. These are even better cause there's gooey caramel on top of them.

FOR THE RICE KRISPIES TREATS™

4 tablespoons butter, plus more for the pan

1 (12-ounce) bag marshmallows

1 teaspoon vanilla

6 cups Rice Krispies®

FOR THE CARAMEL

1 cup sugar

½ cup water

2 teaspoons vanilla

¼ cup heavy cream

3 tablespoons unsalted butter

Flaky sea salt

Generously grease a 9x14-inch baking dish or rimmed baking sheet with butter.

In a large pot, melt the butter, add the marshmallows and vanilla, stir until smooth and combined, and then promptly remove from the heat. Stir in the Rice Krispies® and transfer mixture to the prepared baking dish, pressing down until it's even. While it sets, prepare the caramel.

In a small saucepan combine sugar and water and bring to a boil. Let simmer until it reaches 240°F, about 2 to 3 minutes. Turn off the heat and carefully swirl in the vanilla, heavy cream, and butter. It will bubble up but settle down quickly. Carefully pour caramel over the Rice Krispies®. Sprinkle with flaky sea salt. Let cool completely before cutting into sixteen squares.

ultimate
breakfast

I make fried chicken like five times in this book, but fuck it, here it is in the breakfast section because it's incredible any time of the day. People love fried chicken and waffles, but the real tea that nobody wants to spill is that a piece of French toast is simply better than a waffle because it's essentially a waffle that's been fully soaked in cream and sugar and then fried before you pour syrup all over it. Get a grip and get your head in the game. I wake up at 6 a.m. every morning—breakfast might be my favorite meal, but I don't care about oatmeal. I could eat a saag paneer or a whole Peking duck by 7 a.m. without batting an eyelash. This ultimate breakfast has breakfast-y things, lunch-y things, and scrumdiddilyumtious things (that was stupid, should I take it out of the book? No. I have no regrets). The only regret you'll have is if you don't make this meal tomorrow for breakfast . . . or today if you're in a place where breakfast hasn't happened yet.

MELON *and* HONEY SALAD

SERVES 4 TO 6

Sometimes things in life just have to be easy. This is a simple salad but it's perfect.

1 lemon, juiced

1 tablespoon honey

¼ teaspoon cayenne

Olive oil

3 cantaloupe melons, rinds removed, cubed

Flaky salt

Handful fresh mint leaves

In a large bowl whisk together the lemon juice, honey, cayenne, and a good drizzle of good olive oil. Add the melon and toss until well coated. Sprinkle with the salt, mint leaves, and a bit more olive oil if desired.

SPICY CHEESY SCRAMBLED EGGS

SERVES 8

These eggs are addictive. There's something about the cheese, mixed with the creaminess and just the slightest bit of spice that sends me over the edge.

6 eggs, beaten

Kosher salt and freshly ground black pepper

1 green chili, such as jalapeño or serrano, very thinly sliced

2 ounces cream cheese

½ cup cheddar cheese, shredded

2 tablespoons unsalted butter

In a medium bowl, combine eggs, salt and pepper, chili, cream cheese, and cheddar cheese.

Add butter to a medium skillet and heat to medium. Once the butter melts, add the egg mixture and gently pull from the edges of the pan with a rubber spatula. Continue this motion until the eggs are soft but cooked through. They should be shiny but not runny—about 2 to 3 minutes. Transfer immediately to a plate.

FRENCH TOAST

SERVES 8

French toast is like sex: even when it's bad it's good. In this case it's especially good.

2 cups heavy cream

1 (14-ounce) can sweetened condensed milk

1 teaspoon vanilla extract

2 tablespoons honey

2 tablespoons Cinnamon Toast Crunch Cinnadust, plus ¼ cup

3 eggs

8 slices thick-cut white bread (such as challah)

2 sticks unsalted butter

Maple syrup, for serving

In a casserole dish or baking pan, whisk together the heavy cream, sweetened condensed milk, vanilla, honey, 2 tablespoons Cinnadust, and eggs.

Place the bread in a shallow baking dish large enough to hold the bread slices in a single layer. Pour the egg mixture over the bread; soak for at least 10 minutes. Turn the slices over and soak until soaked through, about 10 minutes more. Really let it soak up the mixture, even squishing it a little bit until it's almost falling apart.

Get a dish set up with the remaining ¼ cup Cinnadust for dipping the finished toast in after it's cooked.

In a large cast-iron or nonstick skillet, melt 4 tablespoons of butter over medium heat. Fry half the bread slices until golden brown, 2 to 3 minutes per side. Transfer to the plate of Cinnadust and coat both sides. Arrange the toast on a serving platter.

Wipe the skillet and repeat with the additional 4 tablespoons butter and remaining bread, dipping each slice in Cinnadust to coat both sides.

To serve, melt the remaining stick of butter and pour over the toast slices. Top with maple syrup. Serve with the Fried Chicken and Strawberry Compote.

FRIED CHICKEN

SERVES 8 TO 10

2 cups buttermilk

1 cup Frank's RedHot

1 cup pickle juice

½ cup sugar

1 (4½-pound) chicken, cut into 10 pieces (If you can't find it prepackaged, ask your butcher to break it down for you!)

2 cups all-purpose flour

1 cup cornstarch

3 tablespoons garlic powder

2 tablespoons baking powder

1 tablespoon cayenne

1 tablespoon dried oregano

1 tablespoon dried thyme

2 tablespoons Lawry's Seasoned Salt

2½ tablespoons Tony Chachere's No Salt Seasoning Blend

2 tablespoons paprika

½ tablespoon ground ginger

1 tablespoon ground coriander

Sea salt to taste

Not all fried chicken is created equal. This sour and spicy brine makes the chicken super juicy so it's kind of idiot proof. Pile it on top of the French Toast, then smother it with sweet strawberry jelly. It will truly make you lose your mind.

In a large bowl combine the buttermilk, Frank's, pickle juice, and sugar. Add the chicken. Cover with plastic and refrigerate 2 to 24 hours.

In another large bowl, combine the flour, cornstarch, garlic powder, baking powder, cayenne, dried oregano, dried thyme, Lawry's, Tony Chachere's, paprika, ginger, and coriander. Add a little bit of the buttermilk and stir it in to make little clumps.

Heat a heavy pot filled halfway with oil over medium heat until a deep-fry thermometer reads 350°F, or set your deep fryer to 350°F.

Dredge the chicken. Transfer to a baking sheet until ready to fry.

Fry the chicken in batches until golden brown and a thermometer inserted into the thickest part (avoiding bone) reads 160°F, about 8 minutes for small pieces and 14 minutes for large. Adjust the heat to maintain a temperature of 350°F during cooking. Transfer to a wire rack set on a sheet pan; season with sea salt. Serve warm or at room temperature.

STRAWBERRY COMPOTE

MAKES 2 CUPS

This is something you should always have on hand. Have fun with it. Try different fruits if you have them. I love plums or a little ginger. Sometimes I just eat it with a spoon. Or on yogurt or ice cream for dessert.

2 quarts strawberries, hulled and sliced

½ cup sugar

1 teaspoon vanilla extract

1 lemon, zested and juiced

1 teaspoon cinnamon

In a large saucepan, combine the strawberries, sugar, vanilla, lemon zest and juice, and cinnamon. Heat over medium, stirring, until sugar dissolves, about 4 minutes. Mash up the berries a bit with a wooden spoon, and let cook until the mixture begins to thicken, another 4 to 5 minutes. Serve right away, or store in an airtight container for up to a week.

pop's food
for the soul

I have a friend named Pop who cooks insane soul food every Sunday. Sometimes you go to his house and there's five people, sometimes there's seventy-five. He has an open-door policy, just no dickheads allowed. We've known each other for almost twenty years and I can't even remember how we first met, but I think it probably had something to do with food. This is a typical menu you could expect when coming to one of our pop-ups.

In 2020, during COVID and the summer of national protests, a man named David McAtee was shot and killed by the national guard in Louisville, Kentucky, while police were attempting to disperse a crowd across the street. He was an incredible chef who owned a restaurant called YaYa's BBQ Shack. No one had anything bad to say about him. He died doing what he loved most, cooking and caring for people. Pop and I were both so distraught over what happened that we decided to join forces with the writer and actor Aida Osman to raise money for David's family. We thought the best way to honor him was to cook, so we started a rrecurring charity food pop-up called Munchie's Food Kitchen. Since we started it, we've raised more than a million dollars for different people and other charitable organizations.

CORNBREAD

MAKES ONE 9X13-INCH PAN

Cornbread is incredible as is, but if you throw a honey glaze on top it's even better, and if you throw brown butter on top of the honey it's . . . ooey-gooey sticky naughty-boi time.

1 cup vegetable oil

2 cups cornmeal

2 cups flour

1⅓ cups sugar

2 tablespoons baking powder

1 tablespoon kosher salt

1 cup buttermilk

5 eggs

½ cup unsalted butter, cut into small pieces

½ cup honey

2 tablespoons confectioners' sugar

Preheat the oven to 350°F.

Pour the oil into a 9x13-inch baking pan and preheat in the oven for 20 minutes.

In a large bowl, combine the cornmeal, flour, sugar, baking powder, and salt. Whisk to combine.

In a separate large bowl, whisk together the buttermilk and eggs, then add the dry ingredients and fold together with a spatula until combined.

Carefully take the hot oil out of the oven and pour it into the batter. Let it sizzle for about 30 seconds.

Pour the batter into the pan and bake for 35 to 45 minutes, or until the middle is set.

Meanwhile, make the glaze.

Put the butter in a small saucepan and heat over medium-high. Swirl the pan around a bit and cook until the butter becomes a nice golden brown, but not too dark! You don't want the little bits in the bottom to burn. Transfer to a heatproof bowl. Whisk in the honey and confectioners' sugar.

Glaze the bread while both the glaze and the cake are still warm.

Cut into 16 pieces to serve.

MAC N' CHEESE

SERVES 10 TO 15

1 pound elbow macaroni

2 cups evaporated milk

1 cup half and half

2 cups sour cream

¼ cup mayonnaise

1 tablespoon ground
black pepper

1 teaspoon salt

1 teaspoon seasoned salt

2 tablespoons sugar

1 stick butter cut into
small pieces

1 stick margarine cut into
small pieces

2 large eggs, whisked

½ pound plus ½ cup
raw milk sharp cheddar,
grated

½ pound plus ½ cup colby
jack, grated

¼ pound asiago, grated

⅓ pound gruyère, grated

⅓ pound mozzarella or
fontina, grated

¼ cup fresh grated
parmesan

½ pound Velveeta,
cut into small cubes

½ pound muenster,
cut into small cubes

½ pound mild cheddar
(fancy grated)

This mac n' cheese is a top-three recipe in the book. Honestly, the whole getting laid section could just be this dish. You might have a heart attack. It literally has pounds of cheese and butter in it.

Preheat the oven to 350°F.

Cook macaroni according to package instructions. Rinse and let cool completely.

Mix all that shit together in a big bowl!!! Largest bowl you have! Nothing smaller will accommodate. Top with the bag of fancy mild cheddar. It has to be the fancy shred to get the right melting consistency (this should be the only bagged cheese). Try and grate the rest of the cheeses that need to be grated yourself because it makes a huge difference.

Transfer to a 9x13-inch aluminum baking pan.

Bake at 350°F for 35 minutes to an hour until the top is golden/red brown. You know what it's supposed to look like. Turn the oven up to 400°F at the end for about 10 to 15 minutes for a crispy brown beautiful top!

COLLARD GREENS

MAKES ABOUT 2 QUARTS

These are not the greens you grew up with, I promise. Smoked turkey necks and a ton of hot sauce and vinegar make them so delicious they almost don't taste like a vegetable.

3 pounds turkey necks

1 gallon water

1 onion, chopped

2 cloves garlic

2 cubes Maggi bouillon

1 tablespoon black pepper

1 tablespoon onion powder

1 tablespoon garlic powder

1 tablespoon Tony Chachere's No Salt Seasoning Blend

2 tablespoons sugar

3 tablespoons apple cider vinegar

¼ cup Red Rooster or Crystal hot sauce

1 to 2 teaspoons red pepper flakes

5 pounds collard greens, stems removed

½ head green cabbage, shredded

Salt, to taste

In a large pot, simmer the turkey necks in water for about 2 hours. Remove the turkey necks, set aside, and let cool. Add the onion, garlic, Maggi cubes, black pepper, garlic powder, and No Salt Seasoning. Add the sugar, apple cider vinegar, hot sauce, and red pepper flakes to the pot and return to a simmer.

Add the collard greens to the broth, simmer until they are extremely tender, about 1½ hours. Start adding salt to taste. You'll need at least a tablespoon of salt.

Shred about half of the turkey meat from the turkey necks and add the meat into the greens. Add the sliced cabbage and cook until tender, another 20 minutes. The greens should have some liquid but not be too watery. If there is too much liquid, continue cooking until some of it evaporates.

POTATO SALAD

MAKES 3 QUARTS

1 cup mayo

1 cup dill relish, drained if from a jar

3 tablespoons apple cider vinegar

4 to 5 tablespoons yellow mustard

1 tablespoon dijon mustard

3 tablespoons sugar

1 tablespoon ground black pepper

1 tablespoon plus 1 teaspoon seasoned salt

1 teaspoon Tony Chachere's No Salt Seasoning Blend

2 tablespoons garlic salt

2 tablespoons onion powder

5 pounds russet potatoes

8 boiled eggs, chopped

1 red bell pepper, diced small

½ cup red onion, minced

½ cup celery, minced

Salt and pepper, to taste

My mom weighs 100 pounds and somehow consumes 32 ounces of this potato salad every time it's put in front of her. I've never had a better potato salad in my life. Make sure to squish some of the potatoes and dice others for the perfect texture. It's even better the next day, so you can make it ahead of time.

In a large bowl, combine the mayo, relish, apple cider vinegar, yellow mustard, dijon mustard, sugar, pepper, seasoned salt, No Salt Seasoning, garlic salt, and onion powder. Stir together until well mixed.

Wash the potatoes and boil until fork tender and the skin starts to break. Let them cool on a rack or baking sheet until cool enough to handle (about an hour at least). Remove potatoes from their skin.

Divide the potatoes in half. Mash half and cube half in a 1–2 inch dice, adding to the large bowl with the mustard mixture as you go. Add the remaining ingredients to the bowl.

Mix everything until well combined. Season to taste with salt and pepper. Serve or refrigerate up to 3 days.

POP'S FRIED CHICKEN

SERVES 8 TO 10

This is the best fried chicken you'll ever have. The egg white makes it extra crunchy and there are no little clumpy pieces that fall off while you're eating it. Every bite is the perfect bite. It seems like a lot of work, but you gotta just trust the process.

FOR THE BRINE

¾ cup kosher salt, plus 1 tablespoon for the seasoning

1 gallon water

½ cup sugar

1 head garlic, halved

1 sprig rosemary

1 sprig thyme

1 chicken cut into 10 pieces

1 quart buttermilk

FOR THE DRY RUB

1 tablespoon Bell's Seasoning

1 tablespoon Tony Chachere's No Salt Seasoning Blend

1 tablespoon garlic powder

1 tablespoon onion powder

1 tablespoon sweet paprika

To brine the chicken: In a large pot, combine the salt, water, sugar, garlic, rosemary, and thyme. Turn up the heat and stir until everything is melted, then immediately remove from the heat and let cool completely. Add the chicken to the pot or transfer to a big bowl or bucket—whatever fits in your fridge! Brine the chicken for 6 hours then rinse and pat dry.

Brine the chicken (again): In a new, clean, big bowl or bucket, soak the chicken in buttermilk for 4 to 6 hours in the fridge.

Rinse off and pat dry.

To make the dry rub: In a small bowl combine the Bell's, No Salt Seasoning, garlic powder, onion powder, paprika, Poultry Magic, black pepper, and salt. Mix to combine.

Drizzle the chicken with a little bit of oil and sprinkle with the seasoning mixture to fully coat. The chicken needs to sit in the fridge in seasoning for minimum of six hours, but it's even better if it sits overnight.

Pull the chicken out of the fridge an hour before cooking to get it up to room temperature.

(continued)

1 tablespoon Paul Prudhomme's Poultry Magic

1 tablespoon black pepper

Salt, to taste

Drizzle of oil

TO FINISH

1 cup yellow mustard

1 cup pickle juice

¼ cup Crystal Hot Sauce

3 egg whites

2 cups all-purpose flour

2 tablespoons Bell's Seasoning

2 tablespoons Tony Chachere's No Salt Seasoning Blend

2 tablespoons garlic powder

2 tablespoons onion powder

2 tablespoons sweet paprika

2 tablespoons Paul Prudhomme's Poultry Magic

2 tablespoons black pepper

1 tablespoon kosher salt

Peanut oil, for frying

Hot sauce and honey, for serving

To dredge the chicken: In a medium bowl, combine the mustard, pickle juice, and Crystal Hot Sauce. In another medium bowl or in the bowl of an electric stand mixer, whisk the egg whites until they reach soft peaks. When you pull the whisk out of the egg whites and hold it up, the tip of the egg whites should still be floppy.

Gently fold the egg whites into the mustard mixture using a rubber spatula. You want to combine the two without beating all the air out of the eggs.

In a large bowl, whisk together the remaining ingredients, for the dry dredge.

One piece at a time, coat the chicken in the mustard mixture, then dip it into the dry dredge. Now you're ready to fry.

To fry the chicken: Fill a large pot with peanut oil. Heat to 350°F. Fry in batches of 3 to 4 pieces, and cook until they are a deep golden color, at least 20 minutes. Transfer to a wire rack or a paper bag. I prefer to eat it at room temperature, but you can warm it up in the oven if you want to. Serve with hot sauce and honey.

RED VELVET CAKE

SERVES 10 TO 15

I don't love sweets, but if this cake is in front of me, I'm ravenous like I've been living in the woods for sixteen years and I just saw a piece of food for the first time.

FOR THE CAKE

2¼ cups all-purpose flour

¼ cup unsweetened cocoa powder (not Dutch processed)

1¾ teaspoons baking powder

1 teaspoon kosher salt

¼ teaspoon baking soda

1 cup low fat buttermilk

1 tablespoon white distilled vinegar

2 teaspoons vanilla extract

2 tablespoons red food coloring

1 stick unsalted butter, room temperature

2 cups granulated sugar

⅔ cup vegetable oil

4 large eggs, room temperature

For the Cake: Preheat oven to 350°F with a rack in the center position.

Line the bottoms of two 8-inch or 9-inch round cake pans with circles of parchment paper. Spray the sides with nonstick baking spray and sprinkle with flour. Set aside.

In a large bowl, sift together the flour, cocoa powder, baking powder, salt, and baking soda. Set aside.

Combine the buttermilk, vinegar, vanilla, and food coloring, and mix until fully combined. Set aside.

In the bowl of a stand mixer fitted with the paddle attachment, beat together the butter and sugar on high speed for 3 to 4 minutes, until light and creamy. Reduce mixer speed to low and slowly add the oil. Mix again on medium-high speed for 2 minutes, scraping the sides of the bowl as needed.

Reduce speed to low and add eggs one at a time, beating on medium-high speed between each addition until combined. Scrape the bowl and beat on medium-high speed for 1 minute longer.

Reduce the mixer to low speed. Add the dry ingredients and buttermilk mixture in three additions, alternating each mixture, starting and ending with the dry, mixing until just combined between each addition. Increase mixer to medium and beat 30 seconds until well combined, then

(continued)

2 (8-ounce) bricks Philadelphia Cream Cheese

1 stick unsalted butter, softened but still cool

1 teaspoon kosher salt

2 pounds confectioner's sugar

1 teaspoon vanilla extract

mix by hand with a rubber spatula to ensure the bottom and sides of the bowl are well incorporated.

Divide the batter into the prepared pans, filling each about halfway.

Bake for 40 to 45 minutes, or until the cakes spring back to the touch and a toothpick comes out clean or with moist crumbs.

Cool the cakes in the pans for 5 minutes, then run a knife around the edges of the pans to loosen. Flip the cakes out onto wire racks and remove the parchment paper. Set aside to cool completely.

For the Frosting: Let the cream cheese sit out for about 20 minutes, until almost room temperature. In a stand mixer with the paddle attachment beat the cream cheese for 1 minute until smooth.

Add the butter and salt and beat for another minute, scraping down the sides. Reduce speed to low and add the confectioner's sugar in about five additions, increasing the speed to medium-high and beating well after each addition. Add the vanilla extract. Mix on low for another 3 minutes, scraping down the bowl as needed.

To Assemble the Cake: Use a sharp, serrated knife to trim the tops of the cakes. Place one cake cut side up on a serving platter and spread with about 1 cup of frosting. Place the second cake layer cut side down on top of the first. Refrigerate 30 minutes until firm.

Use the remaining frosting to coat the top and sides of the cake.

Store in the refrigerator. Bring cake to room temperature before serving.

Cannabis-Infused
ROSE DELIGHTS

Nünchi Citrus
Oolong Boba

NET WT

healthy?

In 2018 I was the most out of shape I've ever been. My face was so bloated I looked like I was in a 12-round fight with Mike Tyson. Your friends always wait until you go through a huge transformation to tell you how great you look, instead of encouraging you when you are in a rough patch. That year one of my friends did a weight-loss challenge and I decided to get out of my comfort zone and joined. We had to get a DEXA scan in order to qualify and I discovered I was 32 percent body fat. I was feeling pretty unhealthy and didn't really know where to begin. I got connected with an amazing personal trainer named Harley Pasternak as a last-ditch effort to lose weight. At our first consultation, I said to Harley, "Look, I just don't want to get too buff," and he said, "Don't worry, I don't think it will be a problem." During the last three to four years with a lot of hard work, Harley has completely transformed my entire body and mind, and I feel better than ever.

I am not a nutritionist or a personal trainer, but I have been lucky to work with some of the best (actually, just Harley, but I think he's the best . . . HAHA!). For me, getting healthier was a combination of eating well, walking, and working out. I'm lazy and want results instantly without doing any work. This is the closest plan to that I have ever tried, but you need to do what is right for your body, and it could look very different for you. I don't have

any injuries or other health concerns, but you may need to consult a doctor or other professional like Harley for help. Please don't sue me for these tips—I'm writing a cookbook! I'm not even a professional chef, let alone a doctor! If you've ever seen a celebrity transform into a new person, Harley Pasternak was probably the magician behind it. He's written books that have sold millions of copies, like *The Body Reset Diet*, but you don't have to read any of those because I'm going to reveal his tricks in less than a page . . . sorry, Harley!

Okay, so here's how I lost 50 pounds:

1. Follow some sort of version of this menu below or look up Harley's approved food. I try to stick to 1400 calories a day but I'm only 145 pounds, so make sure you figure out what is right for your health conditions, weight, and body size. A quick way to figure out how many calories you should intake is by downloading the My Fitness Pal app. It makes it super easy to keep track of what you are eating.

2. Get more than 10,000 to 12,000 steps a day (I try to do 20,000). I work my steps in while I'm taking phone calls, and I even got a treadmill desk so I can walk while I'm working, even in the middle of the night.

3. Work out as much as you are able. Everyone's schedules and bodies are different. I try to work out three to four

times a week, mostly HIIT training. I'm not bench pressing 500 pounds. It's pretty easy. Here's a quick workout Harley has me do (but if you can't do these, some push-ups and sit-ups are great!):

- A flat dumbbell chest press superset with inverted TRX rows: start with 20 repetitions and drop two repetitions per set until you get to 10 repetitions

- Harley's superset with pike planks: start with 20 repetitions and drop one repetition per set until you reach 15 repetitions

4. If you really want to jump-start all of this, before you do anything on this page, do Harley's body reset diet (just google it and it will pop up) or buy the book. It changed my metabolism and outlook on food.

STUPID HEALTHY BREAKFAST BOWL

MAKES 1 BOWL

Whenever I'm on a diet, it always tells me to eat a bad egg white omelet for breakfast so I can get lots of protein first thing in the morning. There are lots of ways to do that. This bowl is low calorie and actually tastes good. But I'm not going to lie to you, pancakes taste better.

1 large egg

Olive oil

1 clove garlic, sliced

2 big handfuls spinach

Labneh or Greek yogurt

Pickled turnips, or red onions

Avocado, sliced

4 slices pastrami lox

Finn Crisps

Fill a small pot with water and bring to a boil. Add the whole egg and reduce the temperature so it's not bubbling violently. Set a timer for 7 minutes and prepare an ice bath. Transfer the egg to the ice bath once it's done.

In a small skillet, heat a couple tablespoons of oil over medium-high. Add the garlic and cook until light golden. Add the spinach and cook until just wilted.

Make a breakfast plate with a little spinach in the center. Peel and slice the egg in half. Arrange the egg, yogurt, pickles, avocado, and lox around the spinach, and serve with crisps.

THE FASTEST FISH YOU WILL EVER MAKE

MAKES 1

This meal is light so make your sprout salad pretty big and you'll feel full. The fries are a good way to trick yourself into thinking you're eating unhealthily. This dressing is available at most Japanese markets, but make sure to look for "calorie half" on the label because creamy sesame dressings have a lot of calories. You would be better off with a little lemon and sesame oil if you can't find it.

4- to 6-ounce bass, or other firm whitefish such as halibut or cod

Olive oil

Kosher salt and freshly ground black pepper

1 small sweet potato

Handful sprouts, such as sunflower or broccoli

Mizkan Sesame Sauce Calorie Half

Yuzu kosho and lemon wedges, for serving

Set your air fryer to 360°F. Drizzle the fish with olive oil and season with salt and pepper. Air fry the fish until it can be flaked with a fork, about 8 to 12 minutes. Carefully remove fish and set on a plate.

Cut the sweet potato into ¼- to ½-inch pieces and toss with a bit of oil. Turn the air fryer up to 380°F. Add the sweet potatoes to the air fryer basket. Cook for 10 to 12 minutes, turning halfway through.

Toss the sprouts with a bit of Mizkan Sesame Sauce Calorie Half.

Serve fish with a bit of yuzu kosho and lemon wedges.

CRAB FRIED RICE

SERVES 1 TO 2

This is a healthy version of thai fried rice. It has a lot of veggies in it but still has the tanginess and spice of something you'd get at a restaurant.

Drizzle of neutral oil

6 cloves garlic, chopped

2½ cups rice, cooked

1½ tablespoons soy sauce

1 tablespoon Bachan's Yuzu Japanese Barbecue Sauce

2 big handfuls greens, such as swiss chard or spinach, cut into bite-size pieces

¼ cup fish sauce

3 Thai chilis, thinly sliced (use with discretion)

Tiny pinch sugar

1 pound jumbo lump crab meat

Handful cilantro leaves

Handful mint leaves

Big handful basil leaves

2 limes, juiced, plus more for serving

In a large deep skillet, wok, or cast-iron pan, heat a little bit of neutral oil over medium-high. Add the garlic and cook until fragrant, about 1 to 2 minutes.

Add the rice and cook, stirring occasionally, until it starts to get a little crispy, about 7 minutes. Add the soy sauce and Bachan's sauce. Add the greens and cook until just wilted, about 3 minutes.

Add the fish sauce, lime juice, and chilis, fold in the crab, and let warm through, about 4 minutes. Fold in the herbs just before serving. Serve with lots of lime.

PB *and* BERRY SMASH

MAKES 1

I would eat this even if I wasn't on a diet. A great way to satisfy PB+J cravings without all the sugar in jam.

2 tablespoons peanut butter

1 brown rice cake

2 ounces raspberries

Spread the peanut butter on a rice cake.

Mash the raspberries in a small bowl and spread on top of the peanut butter.

why do we only have thanksgiving once a year?

I can't get behind the ethics of this holiday, but boy can I get behind the food. I love any excuse to get all my favorite people in the same room to eat until we are ready to vomit, fall asleep on the couch, then wake up and do it all over again. Every year while I'm knee deep in prepping for a shit load of people, I get frantic calls from friends asking how to cook various dishes in a traditional Thanksgiving dinner. So thank you, Stuart, for giving me a cookbook deal because now instead of writing out a recipe 200 times I can just tell people to buy my book. Search no more, this is the perfect handbook for having the best Thanksgiving. Play the hits, not some deep cut no one cares about. Take your time with this one, it's a lot of prep but worth it. I like to space things out and take three to five days to get all my ducks in a row. Don't forget to cook with love and good luck, my friend.

PS: The pot pie is actually better than the entire meal, but you have to make everything else to get there.

STUFFING

SERVES 8 TO 12

This stuffing is one of the greatest treasures in the world. It's essentially bread, butter, and chicken stock. It's a wet, soppy mess and it couldn't be better. Use different breads to create the right crispy custardy texture.

1 (12-count) package King's Hawaiian Sweet Rolls

1 sourdough or sesame boule, cut into 2-inch pieces

1 brioche loaf, cut into 2-inch pieces

1 cup (2 sticks) unsalted butter, plus more for greasing

2 large yellow onions, diced

3 ribs celery, diced

Kosher salt and freshly ground black pepper

1 (10-ounce) package Bell's Poultry Seasoning

1 quart chicken stock

Butter a 9x13-inch casserole dish. Also butter a piece of foil large enough to cover the dish.

Heat the oven to 350°F.

Place the cubed bread in the buttered dish. Set aside.

Heat a large pot over medium-high heat and add 1 cup butter to melt. Add the onions and celery and cook until the vegetables are translucent and very soft, about 10 minutes. Season to taste with salt and pepper and add the Bell's Seasoning. Cook, stirring to combine, until fragrant, about 2 minutes. Stir in the stock and remove from the heat. Let cool slightly.

Pour half of the onion mixture over the cubed bread and toss to combine. Add in more of the onion mixture until the stuffing is very moist, but not too wet. Mash with your hands but don't break it all up! Here is where you'll create all the textures. Always lick your fingers.

Cover with buttered foil; bake until a paring knife inserted into the center comes out hot, 30 to 35 minutes. Increase oven temperature to 450°F. Uncover and bake until the top is golden brown and crisp, 20 to 25 minutes. Let sit for 10 minutes before serving.

GREEN BEAN CASSEROLE

SERVES 8 TO 12

Green bean casserole should be made from boxes and cans. Stop trying to dress it up. Rip her clothes off and get to business.

2 (10.75-ounce) cans cream of mushroom soup

1½ cups whole milk

Kosher salt and freshly ground black pepper

Pinch nutmeg

5 (15.5-ounce) cans cut green beans

1 (6-ounce) package French's Crispy Fried Onions

Preheat the oven to 350°F.

In a large bowl, whisk together the cream of mushroom soup and milk until smooth and well combined. Season to taste with salt and lots of pepper and add a good pinch of nutmeg. Stir in the green beans and 1 cup of the fried onions. Transfer to a 9x13-inch baking dish and scatter the remaining onions on top.

Bake until warmed through and bubbling, about 15 minutes. Turn the broiler on for just a second if you want the onions to get nice and crispy and brown.

SOUR CREAM *and* ONION MASHED POTATOES

SERVES 6 TO 8

This is essentially French onion soup but with mashed potatoes. When Jess and I were making the book, she would always say that I'm way too heavy-handed. When she came up with this recipe, she looked at me and said, "Look! I'm heavy-handed!" She was so proud of herself.

3 pounds yukon gold potatoes, peeled and cut into large chunks

1 stick unsalted butter, room temperature, plus 2 tablespoons melted for brushing

1 (8-ounce) stick cream cheese, room temperature

2 cups sour cream

1 cup heavy cream

8 ounces sharp cheddar cheese

½ cup chives, finely chopped

1 (2-ounce) package Lipton Onion Soup and Dip mix

Kosher salt and freshly ground black pepper

Add the potatoes to a very large pot and cover with cold water by 2 inches. Bring to a boil over high heat. Boil until tender when pierced with a knife, about 35 minutes. Carefully strain and return to the pot.

Begin to mash the potatoes with a potato masher. Add the butter, cream cheese, sour cream, heavy cream, and sharp cheddar and continue mashing until really smooth. If you want to go crazy, add to a food processor or use a food mill. Stir in the chives once smooth and season with the soup mix, salt, and pepper.

TURKEY *and* GRAVY

People are always scared to make a turkey. This recipe will make you confident. I guarantee you won't fuck it up. It's all gravy, baby. It's based off a chicken recipe my friend Josh Blum made me years ago.

FOR THE TURKEY

2 gallons water

5 cardamom pods, crushed

FOR THE BRINE

2 bunches thyme

2 bunches rosemary

2 tablespoons Sichuan peppercorns

2 tablespoons black peppercorns

2 tablespoons cumin seeds

3 oranges

2 cups kosher salt

2 cups sugar

1 (16- to 18-pound) turkey

Prepare the brine: bring water to a boil. Meanwhile, toast the dry herbs and spices in a skillet over medium heat until just fragrant, 1 to 2 minutes. Peel the oranges with a y-peeler. Add the toasted spices and peels to the pot of water, along with the salt and sugar. Once boiling, remove from the heat and add ½ gallon of ice. Let steep for 30 minutes, then strain.

Brine the turkey for 24 hours. Then dry the turkey, uncovered in the fridge, for two to three days.

Set the turkey, breast side up, on a rimmed baking sheet with a wire rack. Let stand at room temperature for about 2 hours.

Preheat the oven to 450°F.

Make the compound butter: In a small bowl, mash the butter, mirin, tamari, gochujang, sesame oil, kimchi juice, garlic, and ginger with a fork. It will look chunky and broken but benny insists this is how it has to be to work. Slather all over the turkey.

Roast the turkey: Cook the turkey for 30 minutes, and then baste the turkey all over using a baster or a brush. Watch the turkey carefully—if it starts to get too dark, tent it with foil. If there are burnt-looking little bits on it, benny says to sort of blast this off with the baster.

1 stick unsalted butter, room temperature

2 tablespoons mirin

2 tablespoons tamari

2 tablespoons gochujang

2 tablespoons sesame oil

¼ cup kimchi juice

2 tablespoons grated garlic

2 tablespoons grated ginger

FOR THE GRAVY

1 stick unsalted butter

2 yellow onions, chopped

¼ cup cornstarch

Salt and pepper, to taste

Turkey drippings

2 cups turkey or chicken stock

¼ cup heavy cream

Reduce the temperature to 350°F and continue to cook until the temperature on an instant-read thermometer inserted in the thickest part of the thigh registers 165°F, about 2½ hours. Baste very frequently, at least every half hour.

When fully cooked, transfer the turkey to a serving platter and let rest at least 30 minutes before serving. Reserve the pan drippings for gravy.

Make the gravy: In a large skillet, cook the butter and onions until the onions are soft and translucent and light golden brown at the edges, about 10 to 12 minutes.

Sprinkle the cornstarch into the pan and whisk. Season well with salt and pepper. Cook for about 3 minutes. Add the pan drippings and stock, and cook until slightly thickened, about 4 to 5 minutes. Stir in cream before serving.

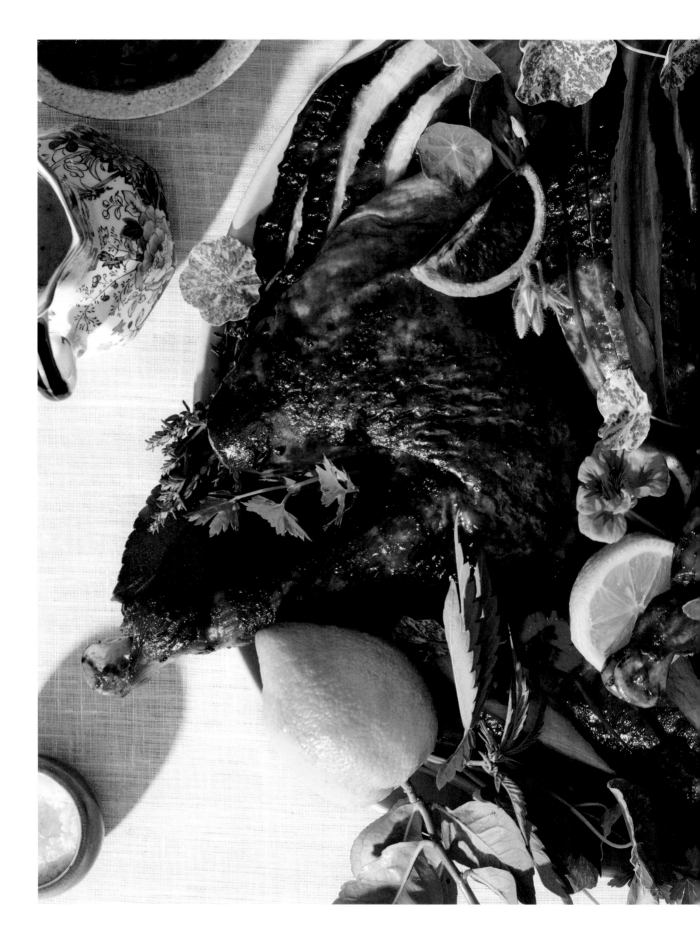

OATMEAL RAISIN CHOCOLATE CHIP COOKIES

MAKES 12 COOKIES

These cookies are truly insane. When Jess was developing these at her house, her boyfriend Ben may or may not have had a sexual experience. When she went to clean the kitchen in the morning, there were crumbs scattered everywhere as if a family of raccoons had rummaged through her cabinets. He hasn't been the same since.

1½ cups all-purpose flour

1½ cups old fashioned oats

1 tablespoon cornstarch

1 teaspoon baking soda

1 teaspoon kosher salt

½ teaspoon ground cinnamon

2 sticks unsalted butter, room temperature

1 cup light brown sugar

½ cup granulated sugar

2 large eggs

1 teaspoon vanilla extract

1½ cups golden raisins, chopped if large

1½ cups semisweet chocolate chips

Flaky sea salt

Preheat the oven to 400°F.

In a medium bowl, whisk together the flour, oats, cornstarch, baking soda, salt, and cinnamon until combined.

In the bowl of an electric mixer fitted with the paddle attachment, mix the butter and sugars on medium-high until light and fluffy, about 6 minutes, scraping down the sides as necessary. Add eggs, one at a time, until combined, scraping down the sides of the bowl. Add vanilla and mix until combined.

Add the dry ingredients to the butter mixture while the mixer is on low speed, and mix until combined. Add the raisins and chocolate chips; mix until combined.

Line two sheet pans with parchment paper. Portion the dough into 4- to 6-ounce balls and arrange on the sheets, leaving at least 2 inches of space between balls. Sprinkle with flaky salt if desired. Bake until just set and lightly brown around the edges, 9 to 12 minutes. Let sit at least 20 minutes before serving.

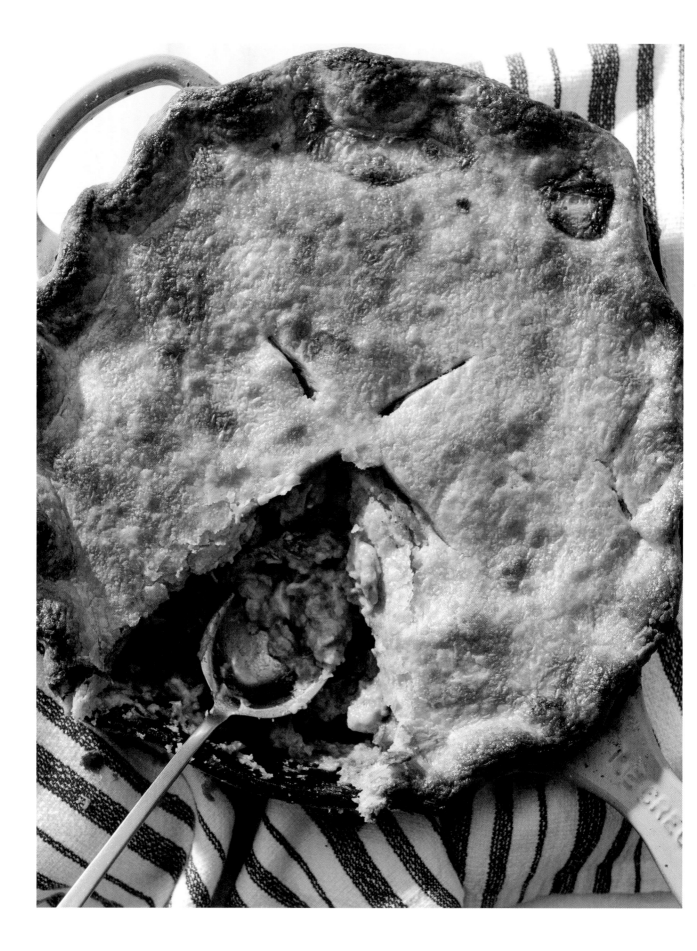

BENNY'S BETTER THAN SEX LEFTOVERS POT PIE

SERVES 8

The best part of Thanksgiving is the day after because you get to eat everything again. This time the leftovers are put into a skillet, covered in cream, topped with pastry dough, and baked in the oven. I'm drooling just thinking about it. Jess made me learn how to make homemade crust for this, and you should too. I promise you, it's not too hard and it's so worth it. In a pinch, you could buy frozen—but try to make sure it's made with butter and not oil!

1½ cups all-purpose flour

½ teaspoon salt

1 teaspoon sugar

8 tablespoons very cold unsalted butter, cut into pieces

3 to 5 tablespoons cold water

2 cups Stuffing

2 cups shredded turkey

2 cups Green Bean Casserole

2 cups Sour Cream and Onion Mashed Potatoes

½ cup heavy cream, plus more for brushing

2 tablespoons cranberry sauce

3 tablespoons gravy

In a food processor, combine the flour, salt, and sugar. Add the butter and pulse until the butter is the size of small peas (about 10 to 12 times). Add the water and pulse until the dough just comes together. Dump the dough onto a piece of plastic wrap and shape into a disk. Let chill at least 30 minutes, up to overnight.

When ready to use, roll out the dough on a lightly floured surface to a 12-inch circle, trimming into a neat shape.

Preheat the oven to 425°F.

Add the stuffing, turkey, green beans, potatoes, heavy cream, cranberry sauce, and gravy to a 10- to 12-inch oven-safe cast-iron skillet. Cook over medium-high heat, stirring occasionally, until the mixture is well combined and thickens a bit, about 6 to 8 minutes. Let cool to room temperature.

Carefully drape the prepared pie crust over the top of the mixture. Use your thumb and pointer finger on one hand and thumb on your other hand to crimp the edges. Cut a few slits in the top. Brush the crust with a tablespoon or two of heavy cream.

Place the skillet on a rimmed baking sheet and transfer to the oven. Bake until the top is a deep golden brown, about 25 minutes.

5 dishes to get you laid and one for the morning after

As a man who looks like Andre the Giant mixed with that one character from *Ice Age* with his eyes too far apart, I've always had to rely on my gift of gab. But I think at this point, my features are so large and grotesque that I popped out of the other side and I'm actually one of the hottest men alive. The power is in believing. And I believe, baby, I believe. I think the best way to another person's heart is through food. It doesn't even matter if you're good at cooking. As long as you give it your all and show someone you actually care, they will have no choice but to push you on the ground and French kiss your private parts.

So here's what you do. Look at the following five recipes. Pick one out that sounds good to you and your partner, or your soon to be partner. Cook it and send me a wedding invitation. But don't forget to buy all the ingredients for the "I Hope We Didn't Make a Baby" Breakfast Burrito, because it's going to happen. Practice safe sex, please.

"PLEASE MARRY ME MARTHA STEWART" LATKES

MAKES 24

If you make these latkes, there is a 100 percent guarantee of a sexual experience. But there's a catch—they make you smell like the inside of a tater tot. And as if the latkes weren't good enough already, spread a little cool crème fraîche and decadent caviar on top with a sprinkle of chives. My coauthor Jess has worked with Martha Stewart for more than ten years and knows I have a secret crush on her. So she invited her over to my house one day. I was so nervous I went out and bought a tin of caviar the size of my head and the nicest champagne I could find, and she never showed up. Jess said she's just playing hard to get.

6 russet potatoes, peeled

2 yellow onions, peeled

2 tablespoons potato starch

1 tablespoon kosher salt

1 teaspoon freshly ground black pepper

2 eggs, lightly beaten

Beef tallow, for frying

Canola oil, for frying

Flaky sea salt

¼ cup crème fraîche

50 grams of your favorite osetra or kaluga caviar, such as Regalis or Petrossian

Minced chives

Fill a very large bowl with ice cold water.

If you have a food processor, use the shredder attachment and cut the potatoes and onions into pieces small enough to fit through the mouth. Otherwise, keep them whole and grate by hand using a box grater. As you grate, add the shredded potatoes and onions to a large bowl of ice water.

Squeeze out all the water with your hands.

Transfer to a dry bowl. Add the potato starch, kosher salt, pepper, and eggs to the bowl with the potatoes and use your hands to mix it all up.

Heat about a half inch of tallow and oil in a large skillet with high sides (I like to use a wok) over medium-high heat until it's really hot. Use a little piece of the potato mixture to see if it's ready—it should sizzle violently.

Use an ice cream scoop to portion latkes and add them to the hot oil, using a fish spatula to squish them down a little. Cook until deep golden brown, about 2 minutes per side.

Transfer to a wire rack set on a rimmed baking sheet and sprinkle with a little flaky salt. Top with the crème fraîche, a huge scoop of caviar, and some chives to serve.

JON *and* VINNY'S SPICY FUSILLI

SERVES 4

¼ cup olive oil

½ cup shallot, finely chopped

1 small garlic clove, finely chopped

½ cup tomato paste

2 tablespoons vodka

1 cup heavy cream

1 teaspoon crushed red pepper flakes

1 pound fusilli

2 tablespoons unsalted butter

Kosher salt and freshly ground black pepper

¼ cup finely grated parmesan, plus more for serving

¼ cup fresh basil leaves, chopped

If you've ever been to Los Angeles, someone has uttered the words Jon and Vinny's *to you. It may not be the easiest restaurant to get into, but once you're in, it's alive. It's a tight restaurant. You're practically sitting on top of one another. On any given Wednesday night, you could be sandwiched between a soccer mom with a bunch of kids and Tyler, the Creator. The food is rich, vibrant, and delicious. If I'm on a diet, I speed past it with my eyes closed because I know if I get one glimpse of the neon lights out front, I'll wake up in a puddle of marinara sauce and rainbow cookie crumbs. They're homies and were nice enough to give me this special recipe.*

"In all of our searches we can't seem to find any recipes that use only tomato paste for this classic Italian American sauce that were published before we shared ours in 2015 with Bon Appétit. Since doing so, it seems the tomato paste method has become the gold standard way (or new standard way or something like that?) of making vodka sauce. In all the tomato paste madness shared on TikTok, Instagram, and Snapchat, we have seen people use alternative dairy and cheese, and of course you can change the shape of the pasta. Make it your own, but tomato paste is the wayyyyyy, and this is our way. Key is good ingredients! Tomato paste method is so good, we heard a rumor that a famous restaurant that's known for their spicy vodka sauce changed theirs to use tomato paste once we published our recipe. No names. But, seriously, chefs should get royalties on recipes and dishes like benny does with his music."

—JON AND VINNY

Heat the oil in a large skillet over medium. Add the shallot and garlic and cook, stirring occasionally, until softened, about 5 minutes. Add the tomato paste and cook, stirring occasionally, until the paste is deep red and starts to caramelize, about 5 more minutes. Add the vodka and cook, stirring, until liquid is mostly evaporated, about 2 minutes. Add the cream and red pepper flakes and stir until well blended. Season with salt and pepper to taste; remove from the heat.

Meanwhile, cook the pasta until al dente in a large pot of salted boiling water, stirring occasionally. Drain, reserving 1 cup of the pasta cooking liquid. Add the pasta, butter, and ½ cup of the pasta cooking liquid to the sauce in the skillet. Cook over medium-low heat, stirring constantly and adding more of the pasta cooking liquid if needed, until the butter has melted and the sauce is thick and glossy, about 2 minutes. Season with salt and pepper to taste and add parmesan, tossing to coat. Divide the pasta among bowls, then top with the basil and more parmesan.

DAVE'S COMPANY CHICKEN *and* COMPANY NOODLES

SERVES 4

This is Dave's favorite recipe. It's called Company Chicken and Company Noodles. His mother always made it when they had company over. He has her cook it for him every time she visits LA. I don't think anyone enjoys this meal besides Dave at this point, but he likes it so much he made it a focal point of a scene in his tv show. When they were filming, everyone was supposed to just pretend they were eating the chicken, but Dave couldn't stop. He ate so much in between takes that he pooped his pants in front of the entire cast. I guess if you are going to eat as many helpings as Dave, wear a diaper.

FOR THE CHICKEN

2 tablespoons unsalted butter, melted

½ cup sour cream

1 tablespoon freshly squeezed lemon juice

1 teaspoon Worcestershire sauce

1 teaspoon celery salt

½ teaspoon paprika

2 cloves garlic, crushed

Kosher salt and freshly ground pepper

4 boneless skinless chicken breasts

¼ cup breadcrumbs

Preheat the oven to 350°F. Brush a rimmed baking sheet with a bit of melted butter.

In a large bowl, mix together the sour cream, lemon juice, Worcestershire sauce, celery salt, paprika, garlic, salt, and pepper. Dip the chicken in the mixture to coat. Cover with the breadcrumbs and drizzle with the remaining butter.

Bake for 45 minutes, until the chicken is cooked through.

In a saucepan, combine the cream, butter, salt, nutmeg, and cayenne, and simmer until the sauce is slightly reduced and thickened, about 15 minutes.

Whisk in the parmesan and fresh herbs and simmer another 5 minutes. Season to taste with salt and pepper and serve immediately with the angel hair pasta.

FOR THE NOODLES

1½ cups heavy cream

4 tablespoons unsalted butter

½ teaspoon kosher salt

⅛ teaspoon nutmeg, grated

Pinch of cayenne

¼ cup parmesan, grated

1 cup mixed herbs (basil, mint, parsley, chives), finely chopped

1 pound angel hair pasta, cooked according to package instructions

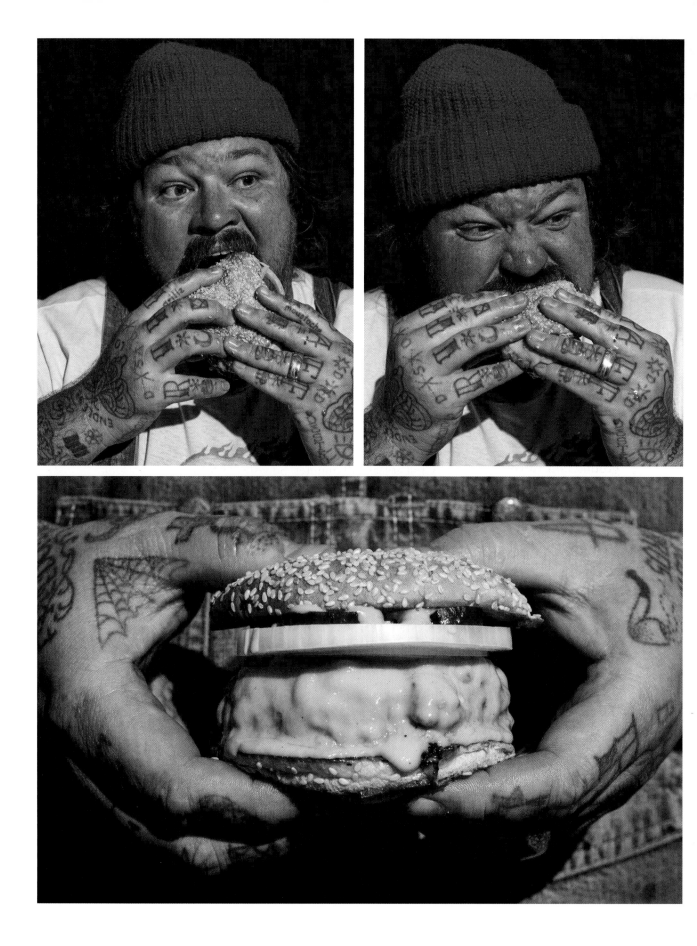

THE MATTY

MAKES 4 BURGERS

This is Matty Matheson's steakhouse burger that made him famous. One time we went to Seth Rogen's house to make some pottery, but first we made these burgers. While we were cooking, we smoked weed that was so strong a few times I actually checked my own pulse to see if my heart was still beating. The combination of eating, smoking, and Seth's infectious laugh made for a 10 out of 10 experience. We made our way down to the pottery studio and got to work. Within the first 10 minutes I became so high that I lost control of all my limbs and didn't even know what I was doing, and somehow Seth was behind me, cradling me like in the movie Ghost, and I felt like it was all going to be all right. I know this doesn't have much to do with getting laid, but if Seth made any advances on me at that point I would have woken up the next day and made him the breakfast burrito.

1½ pounds 70/30 mix ground beef (if you can't get this at your local butcher, 80/20 is okay)

Softened butter

4 Martin's "Big Marty's" sesame rolls

¼ cup mayonnaise

¼ cup ketchup

½ cup French's Mustard

8 slices American cheese

Pickle chips

White onion, sliced

Divide the meat into four equal portions and roll into balls. Chill at least 30 minutes. Squash a little bit until they look like hockey pucks.

Spread a thin layer of butter over the inside of each roll. Heat a large skillet over medium heat. Toast the bun until golden brown. Set aside.

In a bowl, combine the mayo, ketchup, and mustard and mix with a spoon until combined. Set aside.

Turn the skillet heat to high and add the patties. Flatten with a burger press or spatula. Cook until brown on the outside and medium-rare on the inside, about 2 minutes per side. Top with cheese and add a couple of tablespoons of water to the skillet, then cover. Let the burgers steam just until the cheese melts, about 2 minutes.

Set the burger on the toasted bun, smother with sauce. Serve with 6 pickle chips per burger and a fat slice of onion.

SZA'S BANANA PUDDING

SERVES 8

Banana pudding is the holy grail. It's the cure-all for everything. If you have depression, take a bite of banana pudding. If you can't get hard, take a bite of banana pudding. If you don't even like bananas, take a bite of banana pudding. Honestly my book should just be this recipe on 100 pages. One day I was working with SZA at my studio, and she was a little hungry. She went into my refrigerator and there was a little bit of banana pudding left. She took a bite and immediately let out an involuntary scream. Ever since that moment she refuses to come into the studio without a full sheet tray of banana pudding ready, and within two hours it's completely gone. I truly think she would stop talking to me if I didn't make this for her again.

1 (5.1-ounce) box banana flavored instant pudding

2 cups whole milk

1 (8-ounce) brick cream cheese

1 can sweetened condensed milk

4 ounces mascarpone cheese

3 cups heavy whipping cream, or 2 8-ounce tubs of Cool Whip

½ cup confectioner's sugar

1 tablespoon vanilla bean paste

2 to 3 (11-ounce) boxes Nilla Wafers

2 to 3 ripe bananas

Add the instant pudding mix to a medium bowl. Slowly pour in the milk, mixing with a whisk or hand mixer for a couple of minutes until there are no lumps. Set aside.

In a separate large bowl, combine the cream cheese, condensed milk, and mascarpone with a hand mixer until fully blended with no lumps. Fold the pudding into the cream cheese mixture until there are no more streaks of yellow.

To make the whipped cream, combine the heavy cream, confectioner's sugar, and vanilla bean paste in the bowl of an electric mixer (or beat by hand) until stiff peaks form (about 4 minutes), and fold into the pudding mixture (if using Cool Whip fold both tubs into mixture).

Using a 9x13-inch deep-dish pan, begin to make layers starting with a generous amount of cookies. Like, go crazy with the cookies so you don't see the bottom of the dish. Next, add some sliced bananas (roughly 10 to 12 slices). Then spread half of your pudding mixture. Repeat one more time. Then top with one more even layer of cookies. Make it pretty and crush some more cookies all over before serving.

"I HOPE WE DIDN'T MAKE A BABY" BREAKFAST BURRITO

MAKES 2

If you've made it this far, you have to leave them with something to remember you by and what better way than making them a burrito? Unless you want to have a baby. In which case skip the burrito entirely and have sex again without a condom.

1 cup Best Potatoes Ever (see recipe page 135), or 2 store-bought frozen hashbrowns

1 tablespoon unsalted butter

½ small white onion, sliced

1 to 1½ tablespoons taco seasoning

3 slices turkey bacon, or sausage roughly chopped

2 eggs, beaten

⅓ cup yellow cheddar, shredded, plus more to taste

Burrito-size flour tortillas, such as Caramelo

Salsa

Ketchup

Movie Theater Queso and Green Salsa (see recipes on page 121)

Fry up the potatoes following instructions on page 135, or heat the store-bought hashbrowns according to package directions. Set aside.

In a nonstick pan over medium-high heat, melt the butter, add the onions, and cook until soft and translucent, about 6 minutes. Add the taco seasoning and cook another minute. Add the potatoes back to the pan, mix, then transfer to a plate. Wipe out the pan.

In the same pan, fry the bacon or sausage until nice and crispy. Set aside.

Melt a little bit more butter in the same pan. Add the eggs and cheese. Use a rubber spatula to form curds, cook just until set, about 1 to 2 minutes.

Warm the tortilla in the pan on each side, until it's pliable.

Place tortilla on a plate and add half the egg and potato mixtures, and sprinkle with cheese. Drizzle with a little bit of salsa and ketchup. Roll it up, starting with the shorter sides, and rolling up from the bottom.

Add a little bit of butter to the pan. Toast burrito over medium-high heat on both sides until deep golden, about 1 to 2 minutes per side.

Serve with queso and salsa.

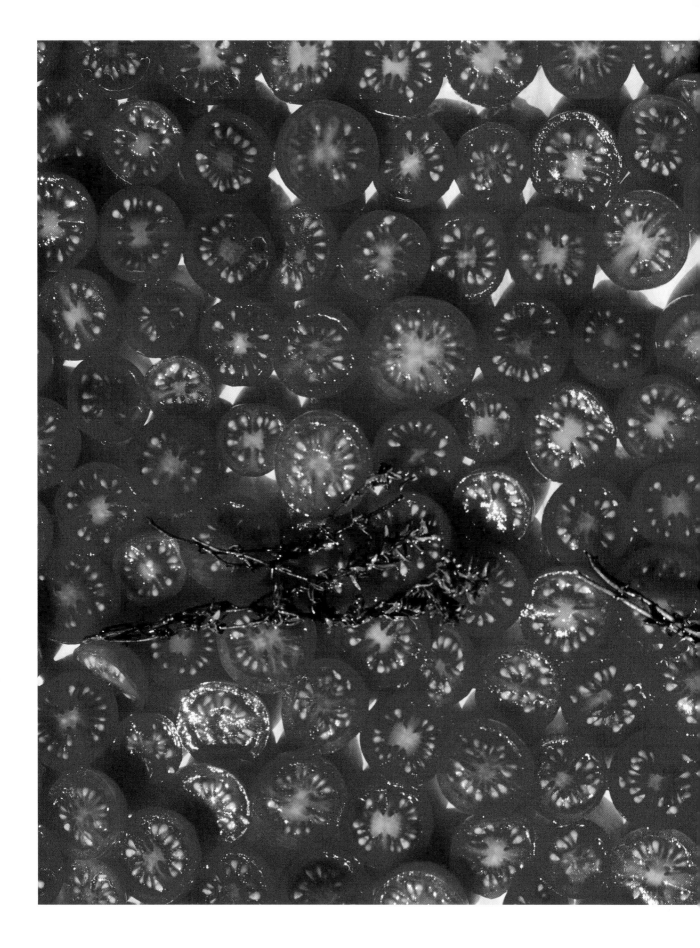

stop asking me where
to eat in ny and la

Every day I'm flooded by calls and texts from people asking me for advice about where to eat their next meal. Usually, they need me to pull some strings to get them a reservation for six people within the next thirty minutes at the hardest restaurant to get into, which I'm willing to do, but I'm a busy man.

Even though I travel all over the country by bus and know where to go in every state, here are my top places in my favorite cities: LA and New York. These are a combo of hot spots that are impossible to get into and holes in the wall that leave you sweaty and filled with joy. Try to hit 'em all, there are no duds on this list!

BEST OF LA

1. Found Oyster: Hip raw bar. Feels like Cape Cod and the East Village had a baby. Eat outside.
2. Sushi Park: Unsuspecting strip mall Omakase sushi. Bring your whole piggy bank.
3. Tacos y Birria La Unica: The best birria queso tacos in town. It's a food truck.
4. Mariscos Jalisco: Go there for the fried shrimp taco—they only have one, you can't miss it. It's a food truck right next to La Unica, so you can do a bang bang.
5. Jitlada: Authentic spicy Thai. Make sure you have a conversation with Jazz, the owner. She's fucking hilarious.
6. Courage Bagels: A lot of people say that this is better than a New York bagel. I'm not picking sides. Expect long line.
7. Lalibela: Incredible Ethiopian food. Get the veggie combo plate.
8. Lunasia Dim Sum House: It's about a forty-five-minute drive, but worth it. Put your name down ahead through an app. Two-hour minimum wait on the weekend.
9. Raffi's Place: It's like a Persian wedding. Don't eat here before you have to do anything. True coma food. Also long waits.
10. Raising Cane's: Fast-food chicken shop. Bathe in the Cane's sauce.
11. Burger She Wrote: Wagyu burger on King's Hawaiian Roll. Just a good ol' burger.
12. Joe's Pizza: There's no good pizza in LA, but this is a shitty version of New York Joe's. Open till 3 a.m. Definitely hit after you've had a few tequilas. Whenever me and Matty go to Sushi Park we wash it down with a slice of Joe's because it's in the same strip mall.
13. Spicy BBQ: This isn't your typical Thai restaurant. It has such unique dishes that you can't get anywhere else. It is very small and very spicy. I am always so full after that I walk 15 minutes down the road and get a food massage while my stomach settles.
14. Sushi Yamamoto: This 8-seat secret oasis teleports you directly to Japan.

The smell of incense mixed with the sounds of Fela Kuti hypnotize you as a beautiful man feeds you some of the best sushi bites in the city. This place is NOT cheap and try to book a month in advance.

15. Holbox: Unassuming Mexican spot located inside a food court. Seafood explosion in your mouth. Get everything.

BEST OF NYC

1. Carbone: High-end Italian. Probably the hardest restaurant to get a reservation at in town. Good luck.

2. Ito: Maybe the best sushi in the country. Bring your first and last month's rent plus security deposit.

3. Russ & Daughters: Historic lox and bagel institution—feels like it's out of a movie. Long wait.

4. Singh's Roti Shop: Make the trek to Queens. Trinidadian cafeteria that looks like a nightclub. Get the doubles with everything on it, shrimp or goat curry with roti.

5. Trinciti Roti Shop: Trinidadian food in Queens. If you're already going to Singh's, go here too and have a faceoff.

6. Peking Duck House: It's all in the name. Get the Peking duck.

7. John's of Bleecker Street: One of the older pizza shops in town. No slices.

8. Rafiqi's Food Cart: Street meat. Or go to any street meat cart in general. Eat this after a night out. Wake up, diarrhea. Repeat.

9. Abuqir Seafood: Make this a part of your Queens trip. There's not really a menu here. Walk in. Act the part. Order some fish from the man at the front. Don't forget the rice and seafood tagine.

10. Joe's Steam Rice Roll: A true Queens gem. Shrimp or beef wrapped in a steamed rice paper that you can see through. Put all the sauces and fixings on. Not a sit-down restaurant.

11. 4 Charles Prime Rib: Fancy steakhouse where you leave 15 pounds heavier than when you walked in.

12. Katz's Delicatessen: A corned beef sandwich as tall as your head. May need to seek medical attention after consuming.

13. O Mandarin Chinese Cuisine: I never go out to Scarsdale and you probably won't either, but my manager lives there and he took me to this place and it blew my mind. It's some of the best high-end Chinese food I've ever had. Everything is delicious.

14. Red Hook Tavern: If you are in Brooklyn, stop by and have one of the best burgers you have ever put in your mouth.

CARBONE'S LASAGNA VERDE

MAKES 1 LASAGNA

If you haven't been to Carbone, you've definitely seen a meme online about it. On any given night you'll see anyone from Rihanna to the president. It's one of the hardest restaurants to get into in NYC, but now you get to make it at home. Mario, the owner, doesn't give out any of his secrets, but I nagged him for two years to let this puppy go. To be honest, this recipe is so complex and difficult you might as well drive to NYC and blow whoever you need to get a reservation. It's worth it. But seriously, try this at home and get a lil taste of NYC and the good life, you won't regret it!

SPINACH PASTA DOUGH

MAKES: AROUND 24 NOODLES

1 (5-ounce) bag baby spinach

7 large egg yolks

3¼ cups (425 grams) 00 flour (Caputo brand)

1 teaspoon olive oil

In a high-powered blender, blend the raw spinach with the egg yolks until smooth.

In a mixer fitted with a dough hook, mix all ingredients on low speed for approximately 11 minutes.

Wrap the dough in plastic wrap and let it sit for at least 1 hour before use, or refrigerate up to 1 day. Pull from the refrigerator at least 30 minutes before using.

To sheet the dough, portion the rested dough into 8 pieces. Keep the dough covered with plastic wrap when not in use. Take one piece of dough and flatten it with the heel of your hand into a disk about ½ inch thick.

Set the sheeter to the thickest setting (#1).

Pass the dough through the pasta sheeter. Fold the pasta sheet back into itself like a pamphlet and rotate 90 degrees to pass the narrow side of the rectangle through #1 again. Repeat 2 times to create a uniform sheet.

Continue to pass the dough in the sheeter while slowly decreasing the setting of the pasta sheeter, passing only one time each. Once you have reached your desired thinness (I stop at #7), pass through two more times at that setting. Cut the dough into 3½x12-inch rectangles. Place cut noodles on a sheet pan sprinkled generously with all-purpose or semolina flour, and sprinkle with flour as you lay them down. Cover with a clean kitchen towel. Repeat with remaining pieces of dough.

If not cooking the noodles right away, cover tightly with plastic wrap and refrigerate up to 1 day.

LASAGNE VERDE TOMATO SAUCE

MAKES ABOUT 6 CUPS

1¾ cups (100 grams) Demi-Sec Tomatoes, chopped (can substitute with good quality store-bought sundried tomatoes in oil)

1½ jarred (80 grams) roasted bell peppers

2¼ cups (500 grams) tomato sauce

Pesto Sauce (see recipe page 252)

Olive oil, to cover

Mix everything together in a medium bowl.

DEMI-SEC TOMATOES

MAKES 1 PINT

2 pounds cherry tomatoes

Kosher salt

1 tablespoon sugar

½ cup olive oil

5 to 6 sprigs thyme

Preheat the oven to 300°F.

Cut the tomatoes in half and place them in a large bowl. Season generously with salt. Add the sugar, olive oil, and the whole thyme sprigs, and toss to combine.

(continued)

Arrange the tomatoes, cut side up, on a baking sheet lined with parchment paper. Place in the oven and bake for about 2 hours, stirring occasionally if needed.

Once the tomatoes are done and slightly dehydrated, remove from the oven and let cool to room temperature.

Cover with olive oil and store in an airtight container. Label and date, and refrigerate.

BASIL PESTO
MAKES 1 CUP

10 cups (112 grams) fresh basil leaves

4 cups (62 grams) baby spinach

3 tablespoons toasted pine nuts

½ cup olive oil

¼ cup pecorino cheese, grated

Kosher salt

Working in batches, quickly blanch the basil leaves and spinach in salted boiling water (5 seconds). Place into an ice bath to stop the cooking process. Remove from the ice bath and remove any excess water using a clean kitchen towel.

Blend all the ingredients together using a blender. Season to taste.

BROCCOLI RABE BÉCHAMEL
MAKES ABOUT 5½ CUPS

1 pound broccoli rabe

4 garlic cloves, peeled and thinly sliced

Olive oil

Salt and pepper

4 cups whole milk

7 tablespoons unsalted butter

8 tablespoons all-purpose flour

½ cup parmesan cheese, grated

Pinch nutmeg

In a large pot of boiling water blanch the broccoli rabe. Place into an ice bath to stop the cooking process. Remove from the ice bath and remove any excess water using a clean kitchen towel.

In a sauté pan, heat the garlic with a couple tablespoons olive oil over medium-high heat. Add in the broccoli rabe and cook. Season with salt and pepper to taste.

Once cooked, remove from the heat and let cool. Once the cooked broccoli rabe is cooled, finely chop and set aside.

To make the Béchamel Sauce, in a small pot over medium heat, heat the milk for a minute or two until hot. In a separate medium sauce pan, melt the butter. Stir the flour into the butter until combined. Continue to cook for 1 to 2 minutes until the paste bubbles a bit, while constantly stirring to prevent burning. Do not let it brown.

Add the hot milk to the butter and flour, continuing to stir as the sauce thickens. Bring to a boil. Remove from the heat and stir in the grated parmesan cheese and reserved broccoli rabe. Season to taste with salt, pepper, and a pinch of nutmeg. Place plastic wrap directly over the surface if not using right away. When ready to build the lasagna, warm the béchamel over medium-low heat to a nice, spreadable consistency.

4 cups Lasagna Verde Tomato Sauce

24 Spinach Pasta noodles with grated parmesan

6 cups Béchamel Sauce

1 cup Basil Pesto

12 ounces sliced mozzarella

Basil leaves

Preheat the oven to 400°F.

Using a 9x13-inch baking pan (or alternatively two 9x5 pans, and you can freeze one for later) layer in the following order:

1 cup Lasagna Verde Tomato Sauce

2 pasta sheets with grated parmesan

2 cups Béchamel Sauce

2 pasta sheets with grated parmesan

⅓ cup Basil Pesto

2 pasta sheets with grated parmesan

1 cup Lasagna Verde Tomato Sauce

2 pasta sheets with grated parmesan

2 cups Béchamel Sauce

2 pasta sheets with grated parmesan

⅓ cup Basil Pesto

2 pasta sheets with grated parmesan

Sliced mozzarella

2 pasta sheets with grated parmesan

1 cup Lasagna Verde Tomato Sauce

2 pasta sheets with grated parmesan

2 cups Béchamel Sauce

2 pasta sheets with grated parmesan

1 cup Lasagna Verde Sauce

2 pasta sheets with grated parmesan

⅓ cup Basil Pesto

2 pasta sheets with grated parmesan

Basil leaves

2 pasta sheets with grated parmesan

Wrap the entire assembled Lasagna Verde with aluminum foil and place it above a baking sheet lined with foil on bottom rack to catch any drippings.

Bake with the rack in the center for 30 to 40 minutes.

Remove the lasagna from the oven. Set the oven to the broiler setting, carefully moving the oven rack to the highest level. Carefully remove the aluminum foil from the lasagna, and sprinkle freshly grated parmesan to cover the top. Place the lasagna back in the oven to broil the cheese to melt and gain color. Let cool for about 20 minutes before serving.

Now, if you really actually made this, you deserve to be praised like a king or a queen and spoon-fed every bite by someone you love, and then get tucked into a noodle blanket and take the longest nap ever and dream of the day when you can just get into Carbone so you won't have to do that ever again.

FOUND OYSTER'S LOBSTAH TOSTADA

SERVES 2 TO 4

Ari's the homey and owns Found Oyster. I go here like once a week. The tostada is my favorite thing on their menu. I begged him for a recipe and he was nice enough to make this especially for me. Raw lobster is a true luxury. The texture is unique, the flavor is just as sweet as cooked lobster, and it's a fun party trick because when's the last time you had raw lobster?

Canola or similar neutral oil for frying

2 (6-inch) corn tortillas

Salt

3 tablespoons tangerine juice

1 tablespoon lime juice

3 tablespoons tomato, finely grated

1 tablespoon red wine vinegar

Dash fish sauce

¼ teaspoon red yuzu kosho

½ teaspoon ginger, finely grated

2 tablespoons shallot, minced

1 raw Maine lobster tail

1 tablespoon olive oil

Fleur de sel

10 baby cherry tomatoes, halved

2 tablespoons cilantro stems, minced

Marigold petals, for serving

Fry the tortillas. Make the dressing. Break down the lobstahhhhh.

Fill a skillet with oil to a depth of 1 inch and heat the oil to 325°F. Fry the tortillas, flipping them over every 30 seconds to help keep them nice and flat. Once the tortillas are a pale blond color and not releasing bubbles, about 2 minutes, transfer to a paper towel–lined plate and season immediately on both sides with salt.

Next, make the tomato vinaigrette. In a medium bowl, combine the tangerine juice, lime juice, grated tomato, vinegar, fish sauce, red yuzu kosho, ginger, and minced shallots. Whisk everything together and let sit in the fridge for at least 30 minutes or up to 3 days.

Place a large pot of water on the stove and bring to a boil. While waiting, prepare an ice bath on the side. Once the water is boiling, add your raw lobster tail (it should still have the shell around it) for 15 seconds, then place it immediately into the ice bath until cool, at least 5 minutes.

With a sharp pair of scissors, place one tip into the shell between the top and bottom sides of the lobster. Cut down both sides of the tail to free the meat. Once you have removed the meat be sure to remove the entrails. You can do this easily by making a shallow incision down the back of the tail and pulling them out.

Slice the lobster into ¼-inch thick slices.

Carefully break the tostadas in half (if you want to share) and place each broken tostada on its own plate. Evenly disperse the sliced lobster, then spoon the tomato vinaigrette over it. Follow with a drizzle of olive oil. Sprinkle with fleur de sel. Add baby tomatoes, cilantro stems, and marigolds.

JITLADA'S MANGO STICKY RICE

SERVES 4 TO 6

Jitlada is one of my favorite Thai restaurants in LA. I've been going there for like fifteen years and haven't even scratched the surface of their menu. When you step through the door, you're greeted by an angel sent from heaven named Jazz. Even if you don't eat Thai food it's worth a visit just to be touched by her infectious energy and magic. I hounded her for their Morning Glory Salad recipe but she said no, so I settled for my second favorite thing on the menu, the Mango Sticky Rice. Thank you, Jazz.

3 cups sweet rice

1 (19-ounce) can coconut cream (preferably Mae Ploy)

¾ cup granulated sugar

1 teaspoon salt

2 mangos, thinly sliced

Wash the rice in a fine mesh strainer until the water runs clear. Soak the rice in cold water for at least 4 to 5 hours, or better yet overnight.

Drain the water. Use a steamer or bamboo basket on top of the pot. Do not let the steamer basket touch the water. Only use about 2 inches of water at the bottom of the pot.

Steam for 30 to 40 minutes, until rice is tender.

Pour the coconut milk into a saucepan and add sugar and salt. Stir until all the sugar has melted and remove from the heat.

Transfer the cooked rice to a bowl. Add almost all the coconut cream—reserving about a quarter of a cup to drizzle on the finished rice—until rice is just wet, and cover with lid for 2 hours.

Serve with sliced mango and the coconut cream mixture drizzled on top.

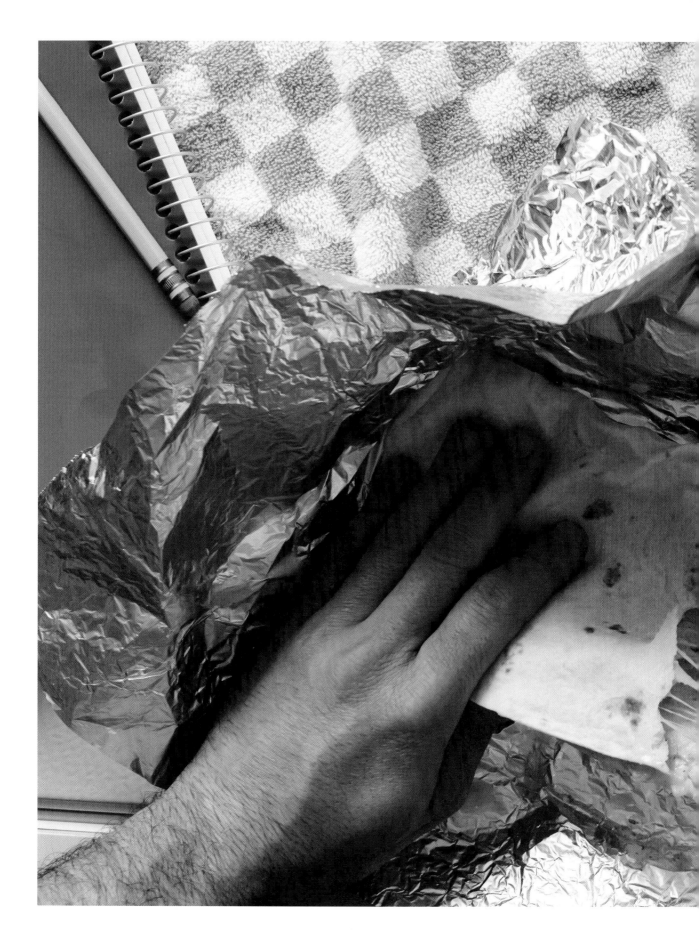

**easiest meals you
can make anywhere**

Everyone always has an excuse for why they couldn't find time to make a meal. My day starts at 6 a.m. and ends anywhere between 12 and 5:30 a.m., or when my body actually passes out on a pillow or the stairs. If I have time to cook two to three meals a day, I promise you do too. No more excuses. Not even if you don't have a pan.

These recipes are so simple a toddler can make them (aka, a stoned college student).

I'd probably sell more copies of my book if I just made this section 100 recipes long. If you're a terrible cook and have no patience or time, this is the section for you. Or at least a good place to get started. If you use Visine twice a week, and the people at Domino's know your order by heart, and you're twenty-eight and still live in your mother's basement, this is also the section for you.

CLOTHING IRON QUESADILLA

MAKES 1

This recipe is so easy to cook. Not only do you not need a kitchen, you don't even need a pan. Just a clothing iron, and it tastes identical to Taco Bell (please don't sue me).

¼ cup sour cream

¼ cup mayonnaise

1 tablespoon garlic powder

½ tablespoon cumin

¼ cup plus 1 tablespoon pickled jalapeño juice

2 tablespoons pickled jalapeños, chopped

½ tablespoon paprika

Kosher salt

10-inch flour tortilla

¼ cup shredded chicken from half a rotisserie chicken

½ cup shredded jack cheese

Quesadilla sauce

In a small bowl mix together the sour cream, mayo, garlic powder, cumin, jalapeño juice, pickled jalapeños, and paprika. Season with a bit of salt.

Place the tortilla on a piece of foil. Spread the chicken on one half of the tortilla, top with the cheese, and drizzle with a bit of the sauce. Fold in half and close up your foil packet.

Put on a heat-safe surface, and iron that baby. You'll need to go for 3 to 4 minutes per side to get it nice and brown and melt the cheese. Serve with more sauce!

MICROWAVE BUFFALO CHICKEN NACHOS

SERVES 1 TO 8

The combination of ranch and Frank's RedHot is impossible to not keep eating. Are we sure there're no illegal substances in either one of these? You make these nachos in the microwave. You don't even need a brain to do it. Lil Dicky makes me keep a gallon of this chicken mixture in my freezer at all times, waiting to be devoured on a drunken evening.

4 cups shredded chicken from 1 rotisserie chicken

1½ cups Frank's RedHot

1 cup ranch dressing (I like Hidden Valley)

2 (6-ounce) bags of shredded yellow cheddar cheese

3 cups tortilla chips

Sour cream, for serving

Sliced scallions, for serving

In a large microwave-safe bowl, mix together the chicken, Frank's, ranch, and 1 bag of cheese. Microwave for about a minute, take it out and stir it, and repeat until it's all creamy and smooth.

Layer the chips and chicken mixture on a microwave-safe platter, and top with the remaining cheese. Microwave again until cheese is melted.

Top with sour cream and scallions.

3 SECOND BREAKFAST SANDWICH

MAKES 1

This sandwich takes less than five minutes to make all in. I don't want to hear excuses. Just mmm after you take the first bite.

2 tablespoons unsalted butter

2 eggs, beaten

Kaiser roll

2 slices American cheese

1 to 2 frozen sausage patties

1 frozen hash brown patty

Ketchup and hot sauce, for serving

Heat pan over high-ish heat to melt the butter. Whisk the eggs until smooth and add to the pan. Using a rubber spatula, push eggs from the edges to the center, until the eggs are just set, about 1 to 2 minutes. Transfer the eggs to the roll and lay the cheese over the eggs.

In the same pan, cook the sausage and hash browns until browned on both sides, about 2 minutes.

Put lots of ketchup and hot sauce on top and eat it!

STICKY ICKY SESAME CHICKEN

SERVES 4

So you suck at cooking but want to impress your friends. You can cook this in the time it takes cold and soggy Panda Express delivery to show up . . . so make the right decision.

3 garlic cloves, chopped

3 tablespoons, plus 2 cups cornstarch

1 egg

1 pound boneless, skinless chicken thighs

A few drops water

Peanut oil, for frying

2 tablespoons honey

3 tablespoons brown sugar

2½ tablespoons soy sauce

2½ tablespoons ketchup

1 tablespoon white vinegar

3½ tablespoons water

3 tablespoons Coca-Cola

3 to 4 tablespoons sesame oil

Sliced scallions, for serving

Toasted sesame seeds, for serving

White rice, for serving

In a medium bowl, whisk together the garlic, 2 tablespoons cornstarch, and egg. Add the chicken to the bowl and toss to coat.

In another large bowl, add 2 cups cornstarch and a few drops of water to form little clumps. This is really important! It makes those nice little crispy bits. Coat the chicken in the cornstarch mixture.

Heat about 3 inches of oil in a deep skillet or wok, or set your deep fryer to 350°F.

Add the chicken and cook until deep golden brown, about 5 minutes. Set the fried chicken on a paper towel–lined plate.

In a large skillet combine the honey, brown sugar, soy sauce, ketchup, vinegar, 3 teaspoons cornstarch, water, and Coca-Cola and bring to a simmer. Once thickened a bit, add the chicken and toss around to coat. Turn off heat. Add about 3 to 4 tablespoons of toasted sesame oil.

Finish with sliced scallions and sesame seeds. Serve with white rice.

**too good not
to include**

I was trying to find a place for this next collection of recipes but they didn't really fit anywhere. I'm not sure if I'll ever get to make another cookbook, so I'm forcing them in here. There is no rhyme or reason, I just cook these things a lot, and I think they are my favorite recipes in the book. Thankfully I put them at the end so you had to make all of the other ones to get here. It's like a magic trick, ta-da!

TORO UNI SEX PLATE

SERVES 8 TO 10

This is what I imagine perfect sex to be like. It has everything you would want in the best sex of your life but somehow it's on a plate of fish. I know it sounds weird, but you gotta try it. This thing is also like breaking the piggy bank. It's only for special occasions.

8 ounces toro, slightly frozen and very thinly sliced

Drizzle of ponzu

Drizzle toasted sesame oil

80 grams uni

125 grams caviar

6 shiso leaves, thinly sliced

Freezing the toro for about 20 minutes makes it easier to thinly slice. Arrange on your prettiest platter, drizzle with the ponzu and sesame oil, and top with the uni, caviar, and shiso leaves.

SHRIMP KATSU SANDWICHES

SERVES 6

SHRIMP

1 cup cornstarch

2 eggs, beaten

1 (8-ounce) box panko breadcrumbs

1 tablespoon garlic powder

1 tablespoon seasoning salt

Freshly ground pepper

1 pound U/15 shrimp, peeled and deveined

Neutral oil, for frying

12 slices soft white sandwich bread

SAUCE

6 tablespoons Bull-Dog Vegetable & Fruit Sauce (tonkatsu sauce)

1 tablespoon Sweet Baby Ray's

1 tablespoon ketchup

3 tablespoons hoisin

SLAW

½ head green cabbage, finely shredded

¼ cup Kewpie mayo

1 tablespoon lime juice (or yuzu juice)

Big pinch togarashi (I like Yuzu Shichimi Togarashi)

There is something about a piece of fried shrimp smothered in sweet sticky sauce topped with a vinegary slaw smashed between two slices of bread that is softer than any tushy I've ever touched that makes me go wild. Make it right now, no questions asked. And if you don't eat shrimp, make it with chicken.

For the Shrimp: Set up three shallow bowls or pie plates. Put the cornstarch in one bowl, beat your eggs in another one, and in the last one combine the panko, garlic powder, seasoning salt, and a little pepper.

Coat the shrimp in the cornstarch and shake off the excess. Then dip the shrimp in the eggs, and let the excess batter drip off. Last but not least dip the shrimp in the breadcrumb mixture and make sure there are breadcrumbs on every little bit.

Preheat your deep fryer to 350°F, or heat about 2 inches of oil in a deep skillet or wok. Carefully add the shrimp and fry until deep golden brown, about 3 minutes.

For the Sauce: In a small bowl, add the tonkatsu sauce, Sweet Baby Ray's, ketchup, and hoisin. Mix until combined.

For the Slaw: In a medium bowl, combine the cabbage, Kewpie mayo, lime juice, and togarashi. Mix together.

For the Sandwiches: Remove the crusts from the bread and pile on the shrimp, slaw, and a generous amount of sauce.

UNI OH BABY PASTA

SERVES 2

I was supposed to turn my book in, and then my friend Simon came over and made me an uni pasta that gave me the exact feeling I get when I orgasm or reach shavasana in yoga. Stay home, eat this, and leave yoga for another day!

2 scallions

Olive oil

Kosher salt and freshly ground black pepper

½ cup white wine

80 grams fresh sea urchin lobes (uni)

½ cup crab, seafood, or lobster stock

8 ounces spaghetti, preferably fresh

3 tablespoons furikake

Juice of half a fat lemon

In a large skillet, slowly sweat the white part of the scallions in 1 tablespoon olive oil with salt and pepper until soft, then add the wine, raise the heat, and reduce until almost dry.

Add another 1 tablespoon olive oil to the pan and add half of the uni, crushing it to mix with the scallions and oil. As it heats and melts, stir in a bit of the crab stock and begin to emulsify.

Meanwhile cook the pasta—if fresh it will only take 3 minutes or so, follow package instructions if using dried. Reserve some of the pasta water before you drain.

Put the pasta into a hot pan with uni sauce and toss to coat, adding a ladleful of pasta water and/or more crab stock to create a creamy sauce.

Remove from the heat and add in 2 tablespoons furikake and the tender green part of the scallions, finely chopped, with the lemon juice and 2 tablespoons of the best quality olive oil.

Serve and top with the remaining furikake, the rest of the uni, and a drizzle of olive oil, lemon, salt, and pepper on the raw uni.

KIMCHI PANCAKES

MAKES 8

These kimchi pancakes are my favorite little thing, they are so addicting and you can make them in 3 minutes. They are perfect when you're hungover or need a second round of food before a big night out. You might want to keep a batch of this dipping sauce on hand at all times, too, for dumplings or whatever!

FOR THE PANCAKES

Neutral oil, for for cooking

1 bunch scallions, chopped

1 cup kimchi, chopped

1 tablespoon kimchi juice

¼ yellow onion, chopped

1 cup all-purpose flour

¼ cup cornstarch

1 cup water

1 egg

1 tablespoon gochujang

1 tablespoon ketchup

1 teaspoon soy sauce

FOR THE DIPPING SAUCE

2 tablespoons Fly by Jing Sichuan Chili Crisp

2 tablespoons black vinegar

2 tablespoons soy sauce

Add ¼ inch oil to a deep straight-sided skillet, and heat over medium-high.

Mix together the chopped scallion, kimchi, kimchi juice, onion, flour, cornstarch, water, egg, gochujang, ketchup, and 1 teaspoon soy sauce until combined.

Add 1½ ice cream scoops (a heaping ¼ cup) to form each pancake. You'll be able to fit two or three in the pan at a time.

Cook until golden brown on the first side (about 2 to 3 minutes) and then flip and do the same on the second side. Transfer to a wire rack while you cook the rest, adding more oil to the pan as needed.

In a small bowl stir together the chili crisp, black vinegar, and 2 tablespoons soy sauce. Serve with the pancakes as a dipping sauce.

MAGGIE BAIRD'S VEGAN CINNAMON ROLLS

MAKES 24 LARGE CINNAMON BUNS

Maggie Baird is the mother to two of the most talented people in the world, Billie Eilish and Finneas. She is a magical woman. We do a lot of charity work together. Whether it's creating produce boxes from my garden to give away to underprivileged families or other fun events around her Support And Feed organization. But all of this pales in comparison to her vegan cinnamon rolls. These cinnamon rolls blew my mind the first time I had them. They are tender and squishy like sweet little babies. Even after baking them myself I still don't know how she does it!

"I have been perfecting this recipe over many years. Tweaking the amount of cinnamon, adjusting the amount of icing. I traditionally make a double batch of this dough recipe for Thanksgiving and Christmas dinner. I use half of the dough for dinner rolls and refrigerate the rest until the next morning when I turn them into cinnamon rolls. Or, if you need a lot, double it and make them all cinnamon rolls. Your friends will love you for bringing them fresh out of the oven to brunch, or, better yet, bake them at their house so they get the full experience!"

—MAGGIE

FOR THE BUNS

3 teaspoons active dry yeast

¼ cup lukewarm water

3 teaspoons Ener-G Egg Replacer (powdered), mixed with 4 tablespoons water (equivalent to two eggs)

1¾ cup unsweetened soy or almond milk, warmed just to lukewarm

½ cup melted vegan butter (I use the stick version of Earth Balance or Miyoko's)

1 teaspoon salt

Sprinkle the yeast in a mixing bowl with dough hook attachment. Add the warm water and stir until dissolved. Add the egg replacement mixture to the bowl. Measure the lukewarm nondairy milk and add to the yeast mixture. Add the melted butter, salt, and sugar. Blend with dough hook attachment briefly.

Add in the flour one cup at a time, beating until smooth after each addition. Use the last cup only as much as needed. I usually use around 5½ cups, but depending on the weather or the quality of the flour, I might use more or less. The dough will be soft, but still a bit sticky. Knead with the dough attachment for a few minutes until the dough is smooth-ish. You may need to turn out the dough onto a lightly floured surface and knead by hand a few times.

(continued)

½ cup vegan sugar

5 to 6 cups all-purpose flour (the amount can vary due to weather, etc.)

Vegan butter, for the bowl

FOR THE FILLING

½ cup vegan butter, semi melted, plus more for greasing

¾ cup sugar

2½ tablespoons cinnamon

FOR THE ICING

1 cup vegan butter, room temperature

9 cups confectioner's sugar, plus ⅓ cup additional, if necessary

⅔ cup unsweetened almond, soy, or other nondairy milk

1½ teaspoons vanilla

Coat a bowl with vegan butter and add the dough, turning once to coat, and let rise in a warm place until almost doubled in bulk (1½ to 2 hours).

Punch down the dough to remove any air. Divide into two parts (four parts if a double batch). Wrap each in a large stasher bag coated inside with vegan butter and chill fully, which can take several hours or can be overnight. When it's time to shape the rolls (about two hours before you plan to bake them) take out one section at a time.

To make the filling, soften the vegan butter by microwaving for about 10 seconds (it melts quicker than regular butter). Mix together the sugar and cinnamon. Lightly coat the bottom and sides of two 9x13-inch pans with softened vegan butter. Set aside. Roll out each section of dough one at a time into a roughly 18x11-inch rectangle approximately ¼-inch thick.

Spread with half the cinnamon butter filling, leaving about ½-inch border (an offset spatula or back of a large spoon works great for this). Roll up jelly-roll style, starting on the long side of the rectangle, being careful not to roll too tight. With a serrated knife, saw gently with no pressure. Trim the edges and slice into twelve 1½-inch slices.

Place them in the baking pans. Don't crowd them! Allow enough room for the second rise.

Repeat with the other half of the dough.

Cover with a cloth and let rise again in a warm place until doubled in size.

This will take between one and two hours, depending on how warm your kitchen is. Cold pans and kitchen counters can slow down this process.

Preheat the oven to 400°F. Make sure your heat has fully reached this temperature before adding your cinnamon rolls.

Bake until just done. This is a visual thing, but it is only about 10 to 15 minutes, just barely beginning to brown in some places and cooked but still tender! Don't rely on time. Pay attention!

While they are baking, combine all of the icing ingredients in a mixing bowl (definitely use the splatter shield) and beat with whisk attachment or paddle until smooth and fluffy.

After removing rolls from the oven and allowing to cool for at least 20 minutes, use an ice cream scoop or large spoon to top each roll with the icing. Use a metal cake spatula to spread the icing evenly.

Make some coffee and eat! These are magical straight out of the oven, but they reheat beautifully, so if you are lucky enough to have some left over, freeze them. When you are ready to reheat, you can do so either in a hot oven or in a microwave (approximately 20 to 30 seconds from frozen to perfect).

BTS CAKE

MAKES 12 TO 16

FOR THE CAKE

4½ cups cake flour, plus more for the cake pans

2 tablespoons baking powder

1½ teaspoons salt

1½ cups whole milk

9 large egg whites

1 tablespoon vanilla extract

2 sticks unsalted butter, room temperature, plus more for the cake pans

2¼ cups sugar

15 to 20 drops Violet and Royal Purple Gel food coloring

FOR THE FROSTING

8 sticks unsalted butter, room temperature

12 cups confectioner's sugar

1 tablespoon vanilla extract

Pinch of salt

Violet and Royal Purple Gel food coloring

White fondant

Sanding sugar

Sprinkles

I was lucky enough to collaborate with BTS on a song called "Bad Decisions." In our music video, I expressed how big a fan I am of their music by baking them a cake to show my appreciation, but somehow everything went wrong. BTS has the most loyal fans in the world, so I thought it was only right for me to give the army my exact recipe from the music video. Make it at home! Have fun! Send me pix! I love you guys!

Preheat the oven to 350°F. Grease four 8-inch round cake pans with butter, and then add some flour to the pan and tap it around the edges to coat. Tap the pans on the counter and dump out any excess flour. Set aside.

In a medium bowl, whisk together flour, baking powder, and salt. Set aside.

In another medium bowl, whisk together the whole milk, egg whites, and vanilla. Set aside.

In the bowl of an electric mixer fitted with a paddle attachment, beat the butter on medium-high until beginning to get light and fluffy, about 6 minutes. Gradually add the sugar and continue beating until very light and fluffy, about 4 minutes. Scrape down the sides of the bowl as necessary.

Add ⅓ of the flour mixture and give it a little mix on low, then add ⅓ of the milk mixture and beat just until incorporated. Do this again, twice, until everything is fully mixed in. Make sure to scrape down the sides of the bowl, and you can give a good stir by hand to finish mixing. Add the food coloring, and mix again to combine.

Divide the batter evenly between the prepared pans. Smooth the surface and bake until a toothpick inserted in the center comes out clean, about 25 to 30 minutes.

Let the cakes cool in the cake pans on wire racks for 5 to 10 minutes before turning out to cool completely before decorating.

To make the frosting, add the butter and 3 cups of the sugar to the bowl of an electric stand mixer fitted with the paddle attachment. Beat on medium speed until combined, about 8 minutes. With the mixer on medium-low, gradually add the rest of the sugar, one cup at a time. Once it's all incorporated raise the speed to medium-high and add the vanilla and pinch of salt. Reserve about 2 cups of the frosting and set aside. Add the food coloring to the remaining frosting until the desired color is achieved.

To assemble the cake, place one of the cake layers on a serving plate. Spread the bottom layer with about 1 cup of the white frosting, enough to make a ¼-inch to ½-inch-thick layer. Center the second layer bottom-side up (for a flat top) over the frosted layer and press gently to set it in place. Repeat with the third and fourth layers.

Next you'll need to make a crumb coat. Using the remaining white frosting, create a very thin layer around the sides of the cake and then along the top. Refrigerate for at least 30 minutes, up to overnight.

Once the cake is chilled, frost the cake with the purple frosting. Use a large offset spatula to create smooth sides and a smooth top. Make a BTS logo out of fondant and sprinkle with purple sanding sugar and sprinkles. Place on the top of the cake.

ED SHEERAN'S FRIED ROLEX

MAKES 1

One time, @cookingwithlynja and I decided to deep-fry the $16,500 Rolex Ed Sheeran gave me. I'm not recommending you do it too, but if you're insane enough, or just happen to have an extra watch from Ed Sheeran laying around, let me at least tell you how to do it the right way.

1 cup Italian breadcrumbs

½ tablespoon kosher salt

½ tablespoon freshly ground pepper

½ cup grated parmesan cheese

2 eggs

¼ cup water

Neutral oil, for frying

Lemon wedges, for serving

Cocktail sauce, for serving

In a large shallow bowl, pie plate, or cake pan, mix together the breadcrumbs, salt, pepper, and parmesan cheese. In another similar bowl or vessel, add eggs and water, and whisk until well combined.

Keeping one hand dry, use one hand to season the Rolex with salt and pepper, and then transfer it to the egg mixture. Make sure it is completely coated with egg, and let the excess drip off for a moment before dunking it into the breadcrumbs.

In a large skillet, heat the oil to 375°F. Throw a couple of breadcrumbs into the pan—you're ready to start cooking if they sizzle. Add the Rolex, and adjust the heat so that none of the breadcrumbs or butter solids burn, you want to keep it at a steady medium. The watch will take about 4 minutes per side. Transfer to a paper towel–lined plate to cool slightly to do whatever the fuck you're going to do with a fried Rolex.